MANDALA
ART

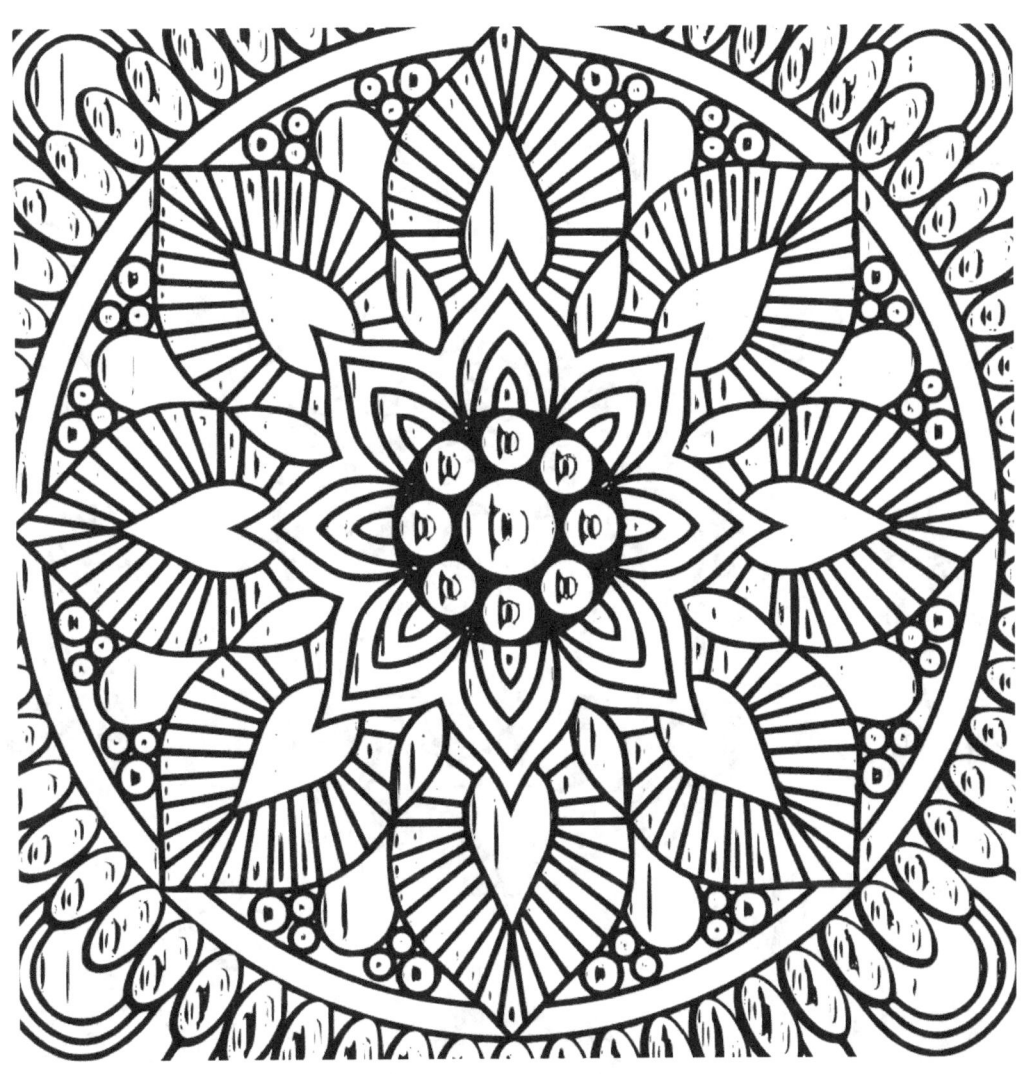

MANDALA
ART

MANDALA

ART

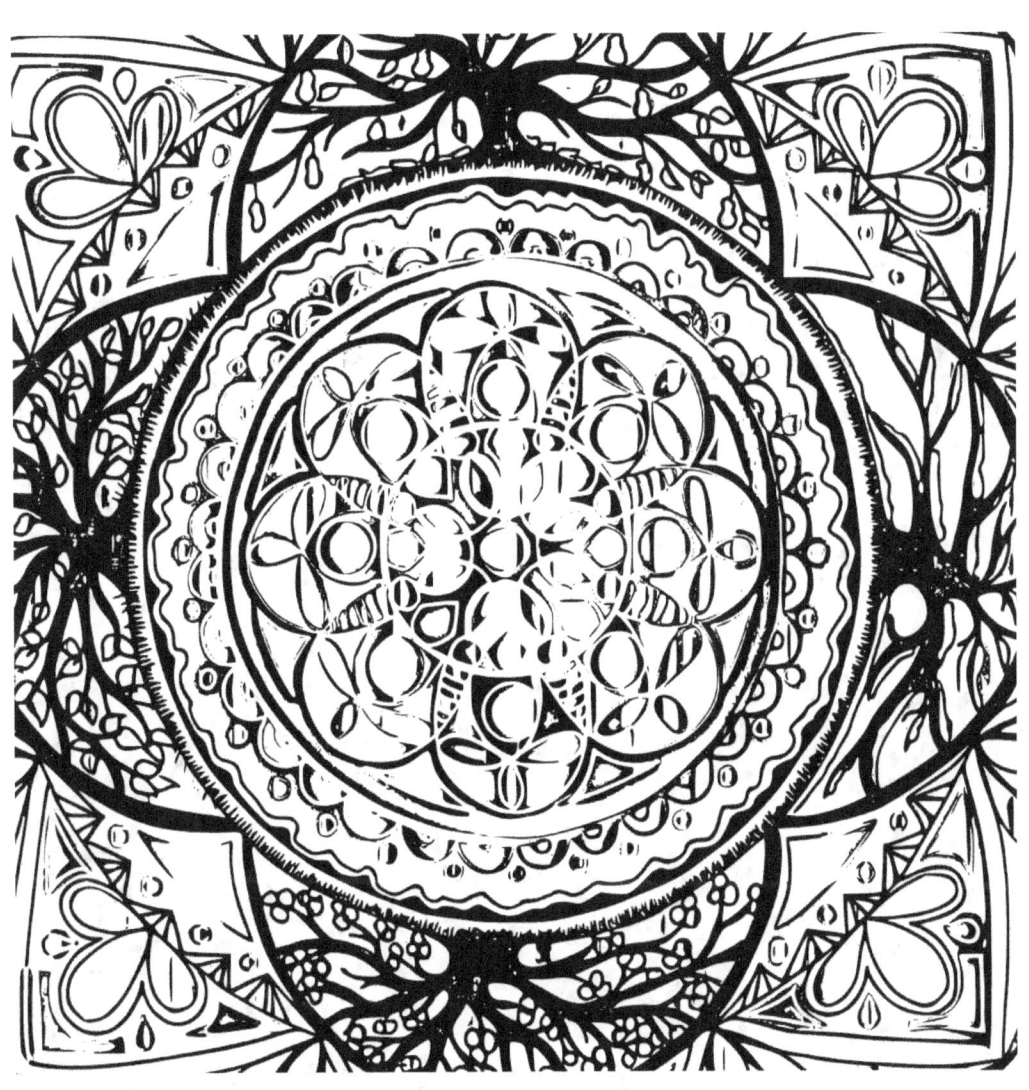

MANDALA
ART

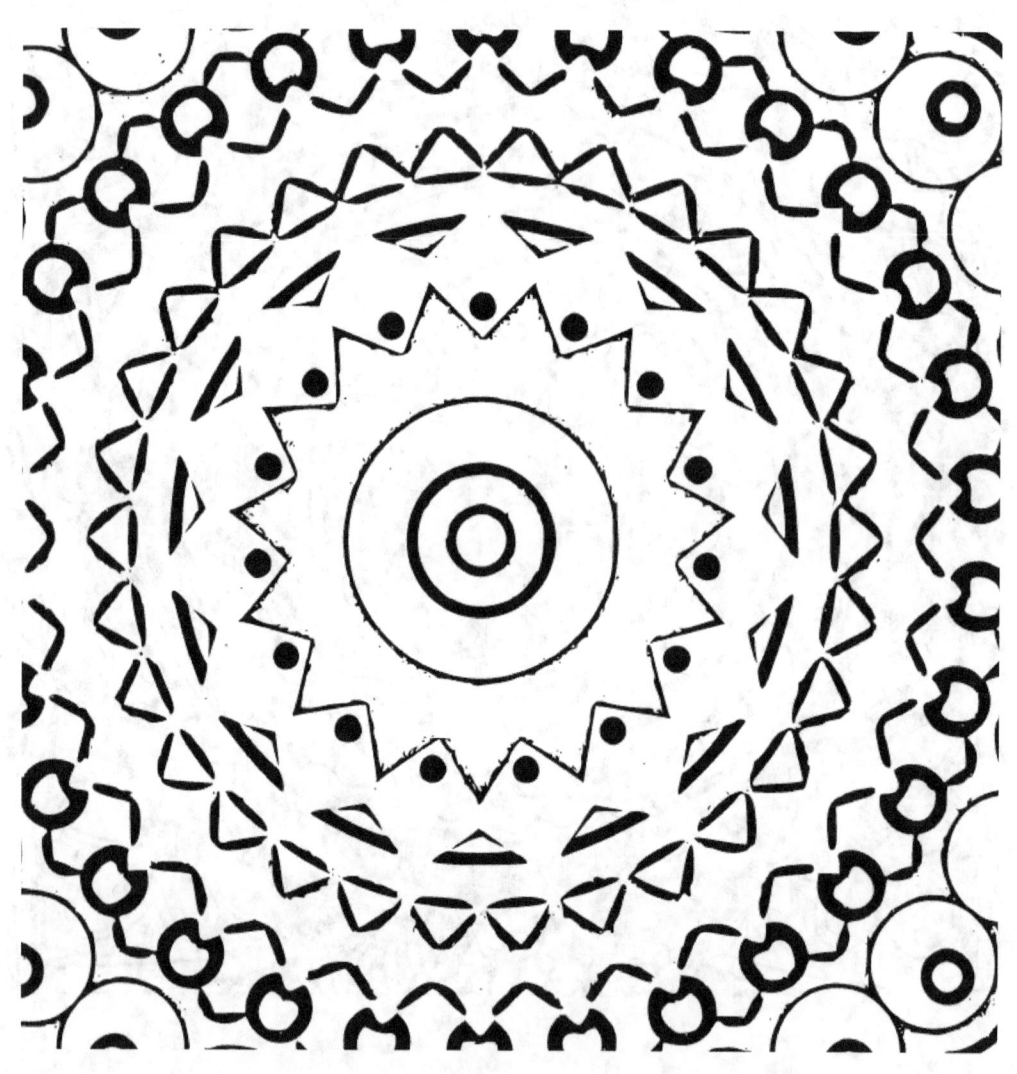

MANDALA
ART

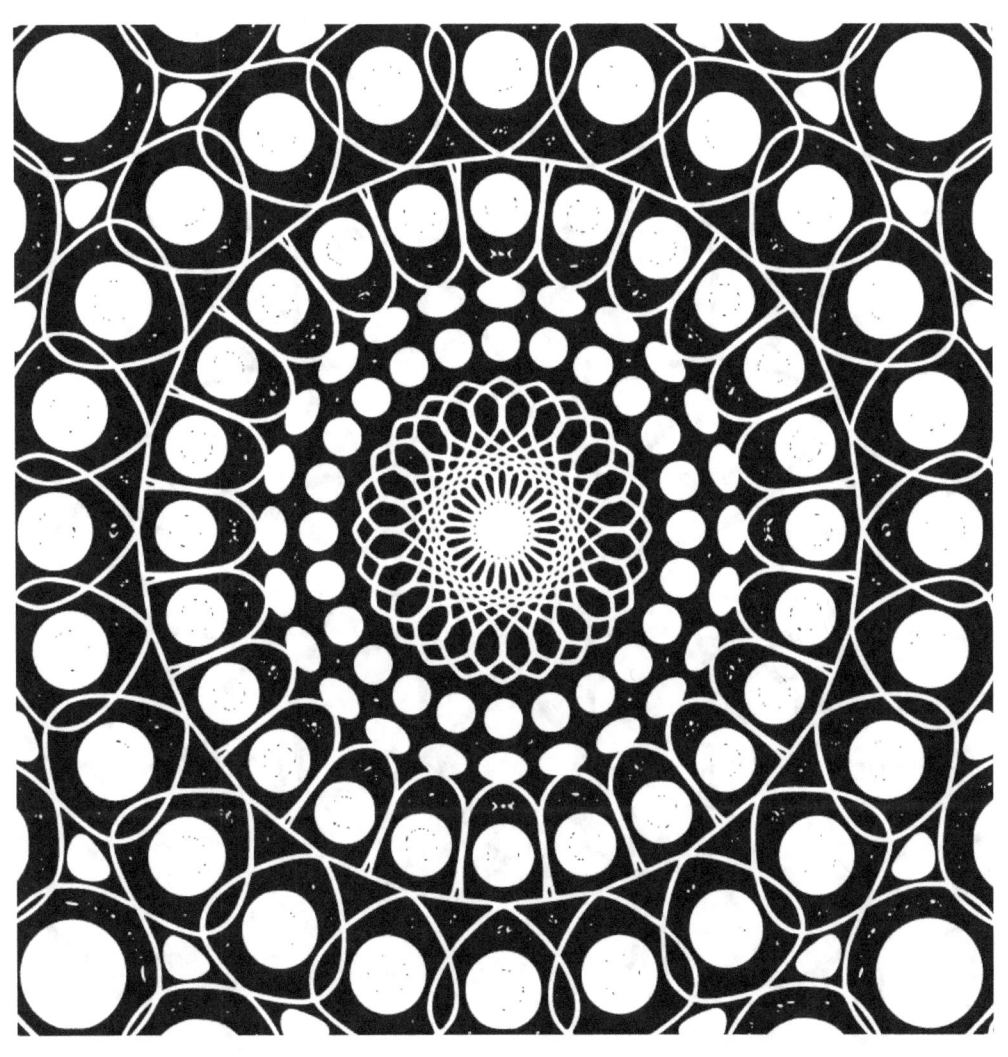

MANDALA
ART

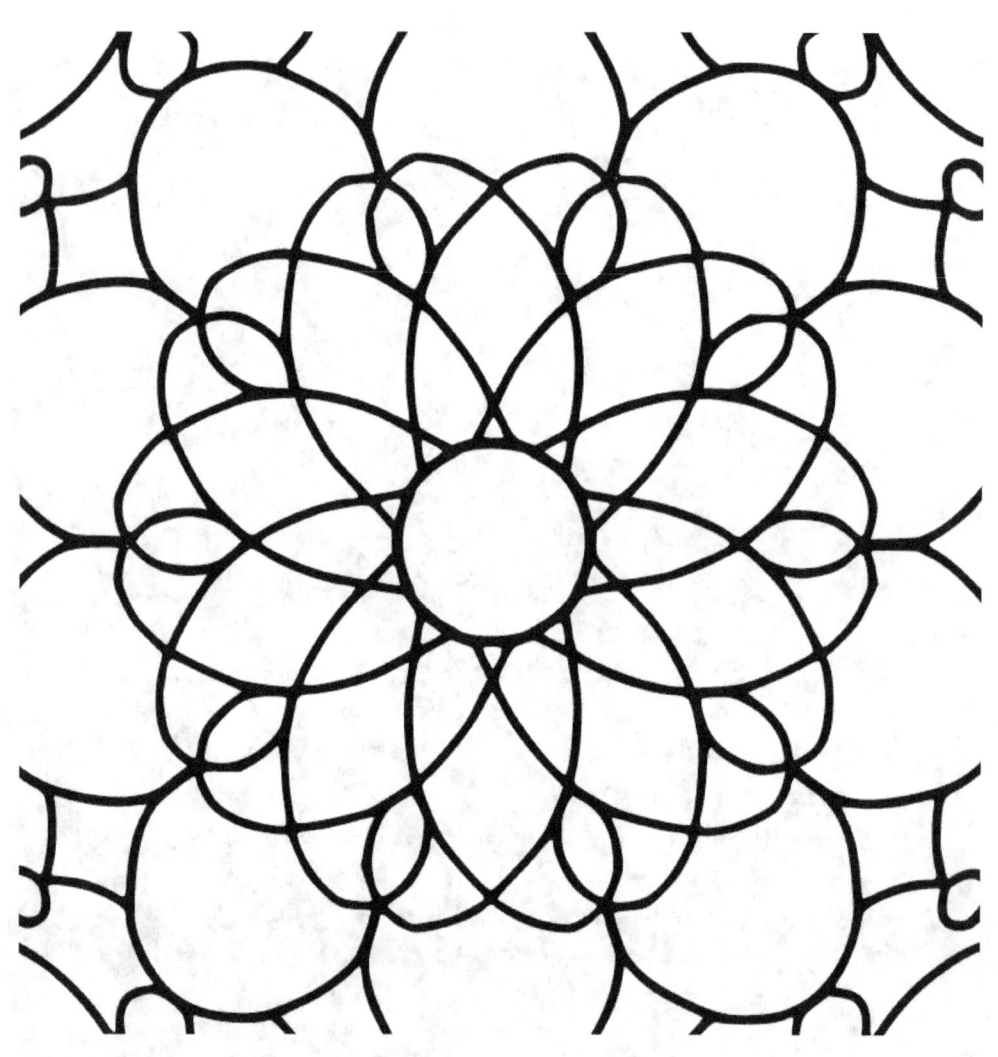

MANDALA
ART

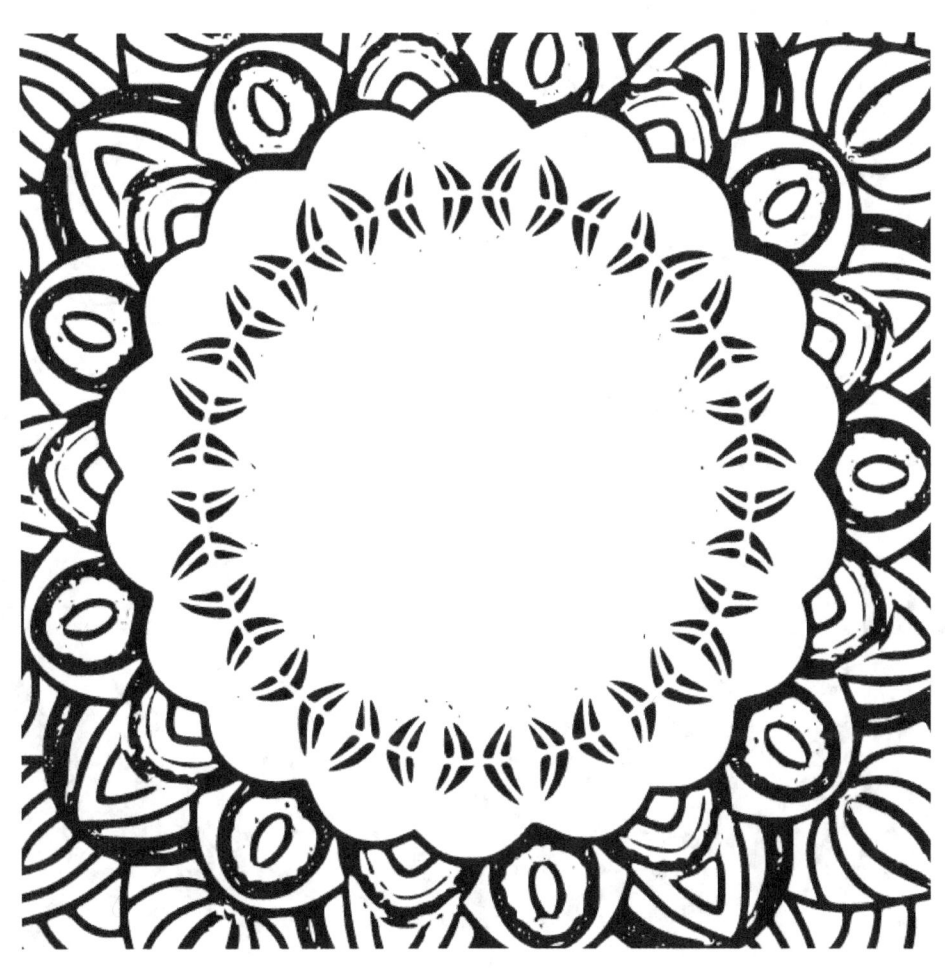

MANDALA
ART

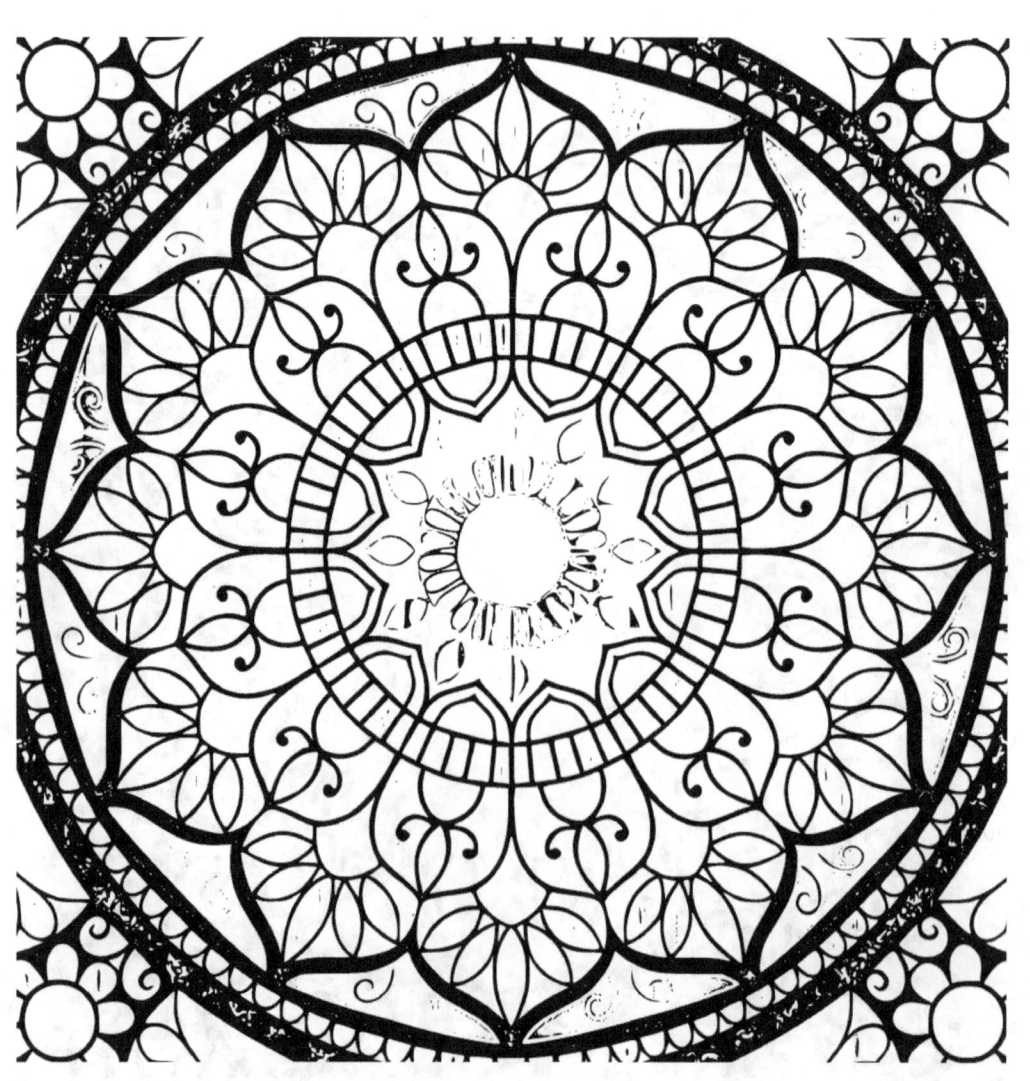

MANDALA

ART

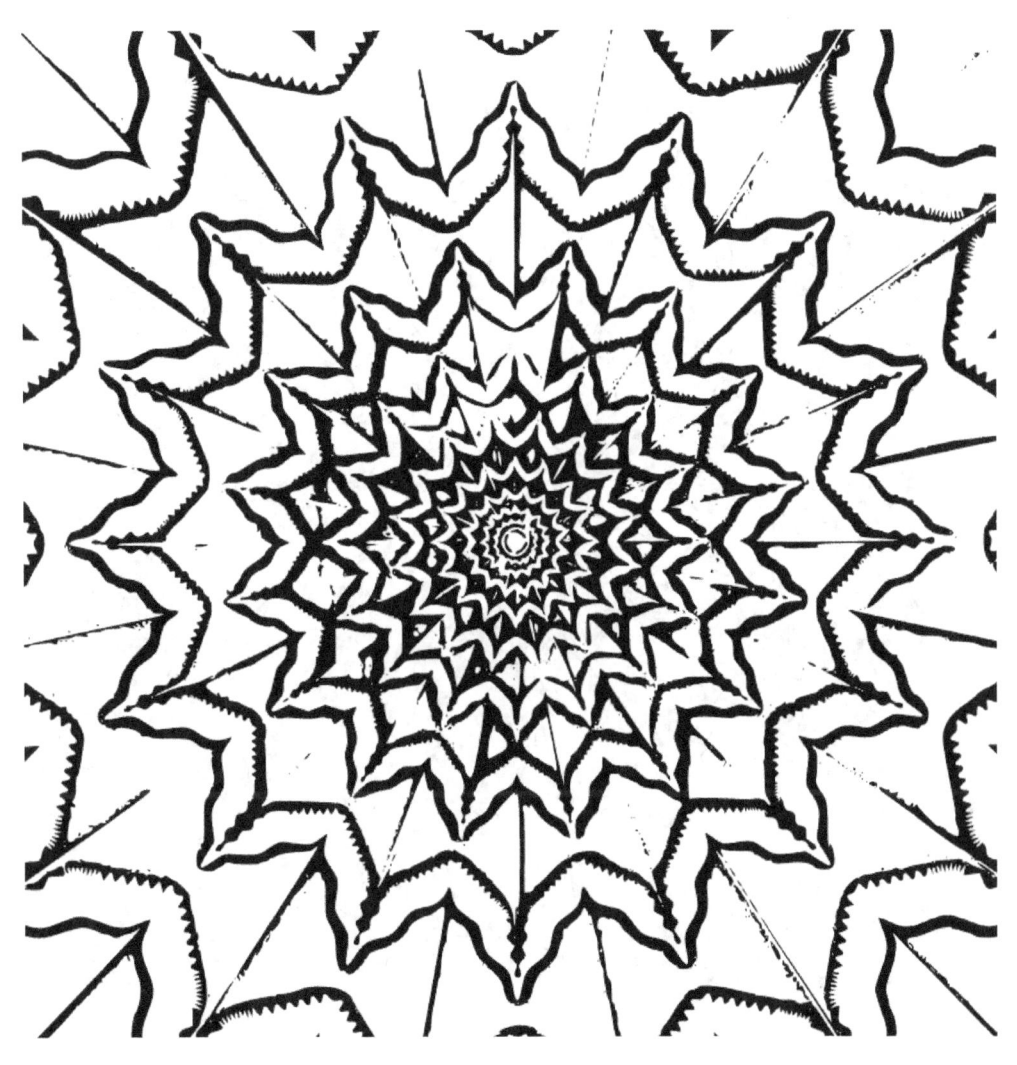

MANDALA
ART

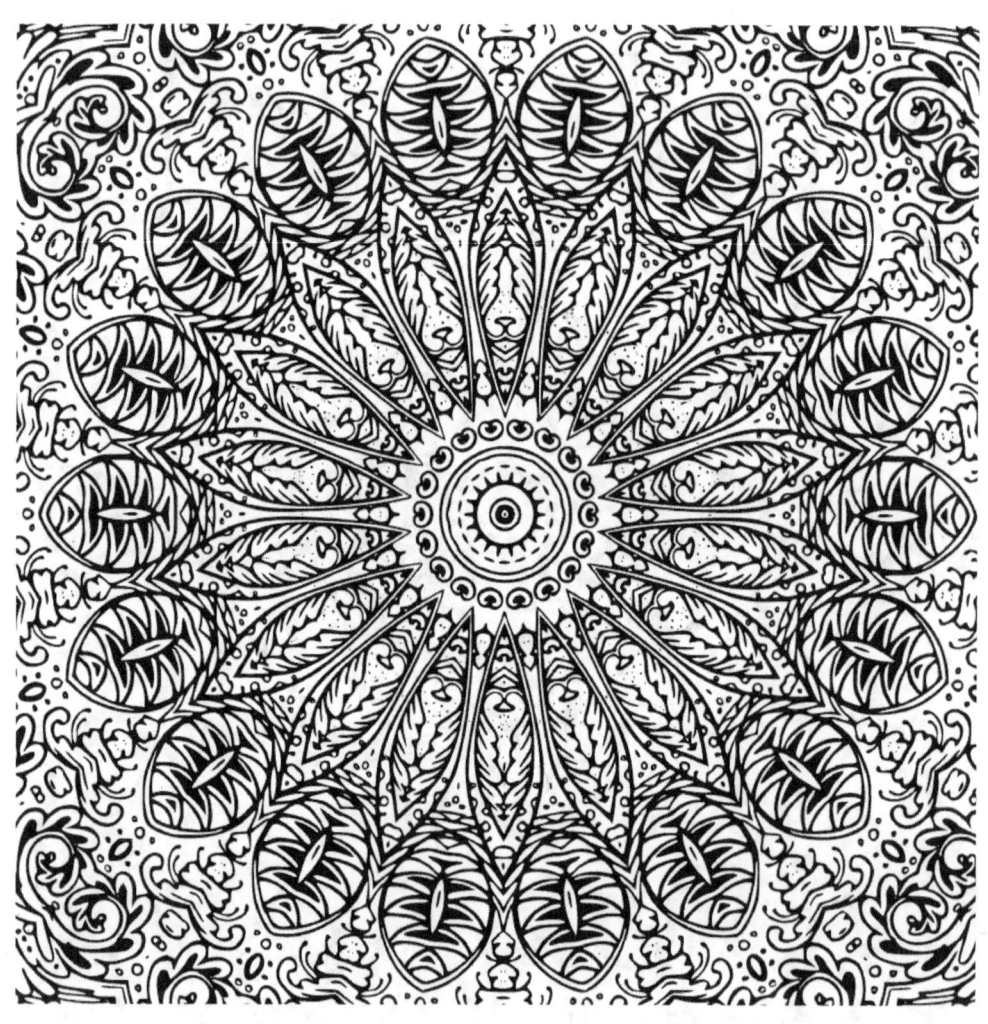

MANDALA

ART

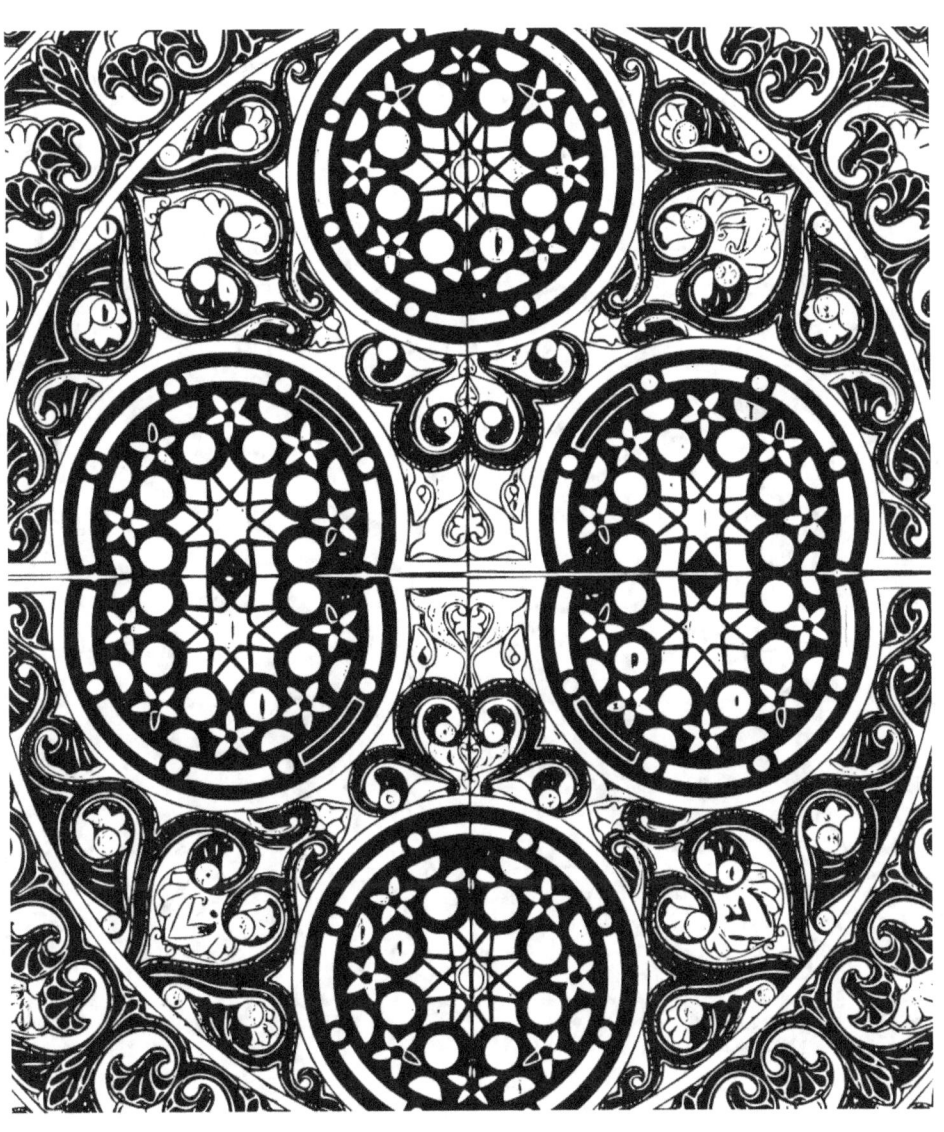

MANDALA
ART

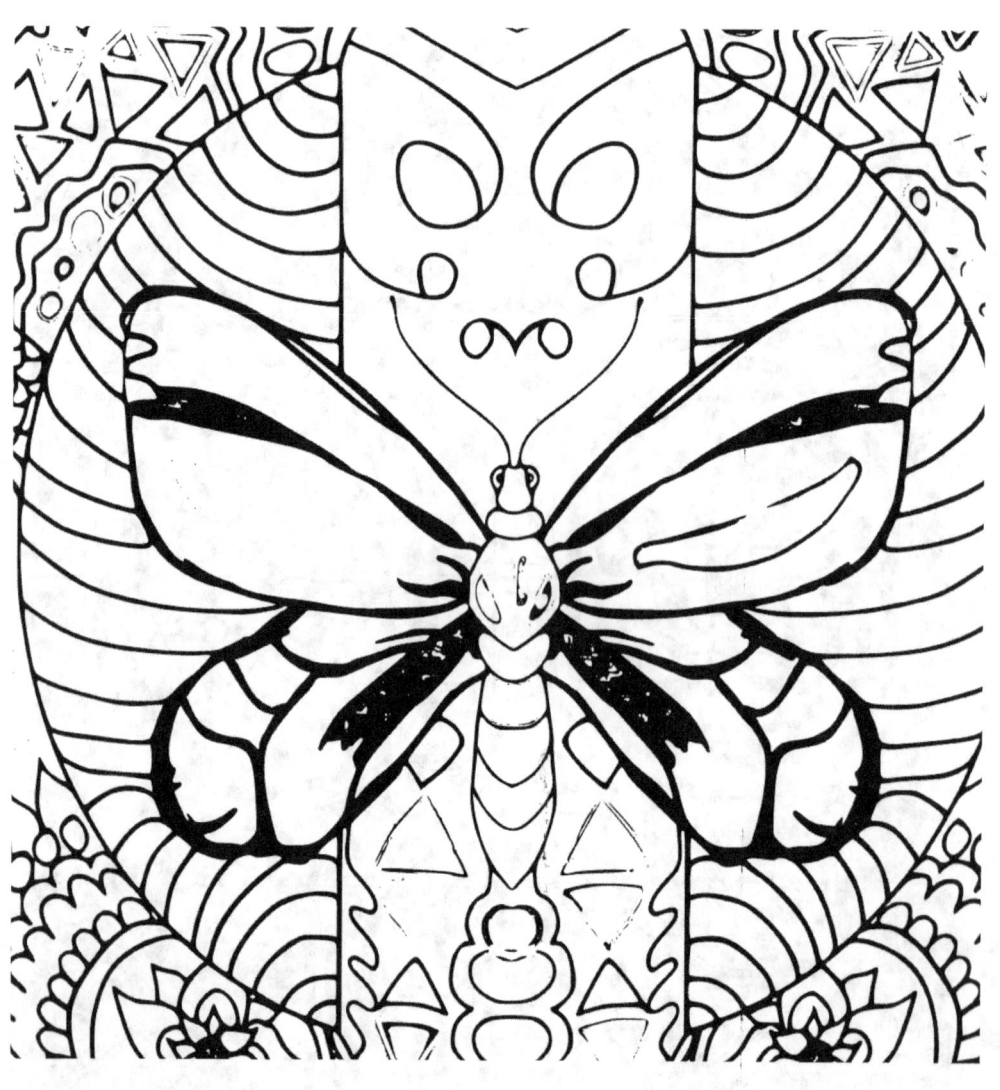

MANDALA

ART

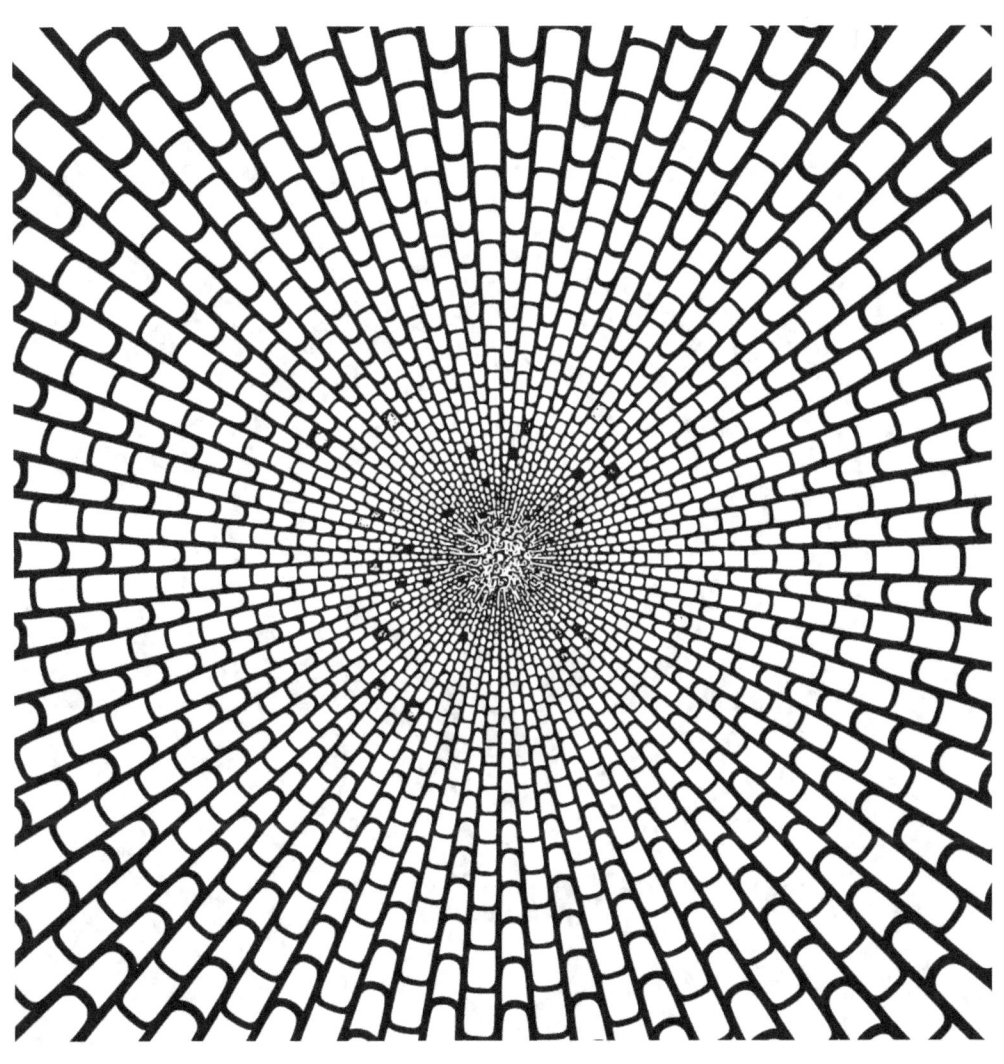

MANDALA
ART

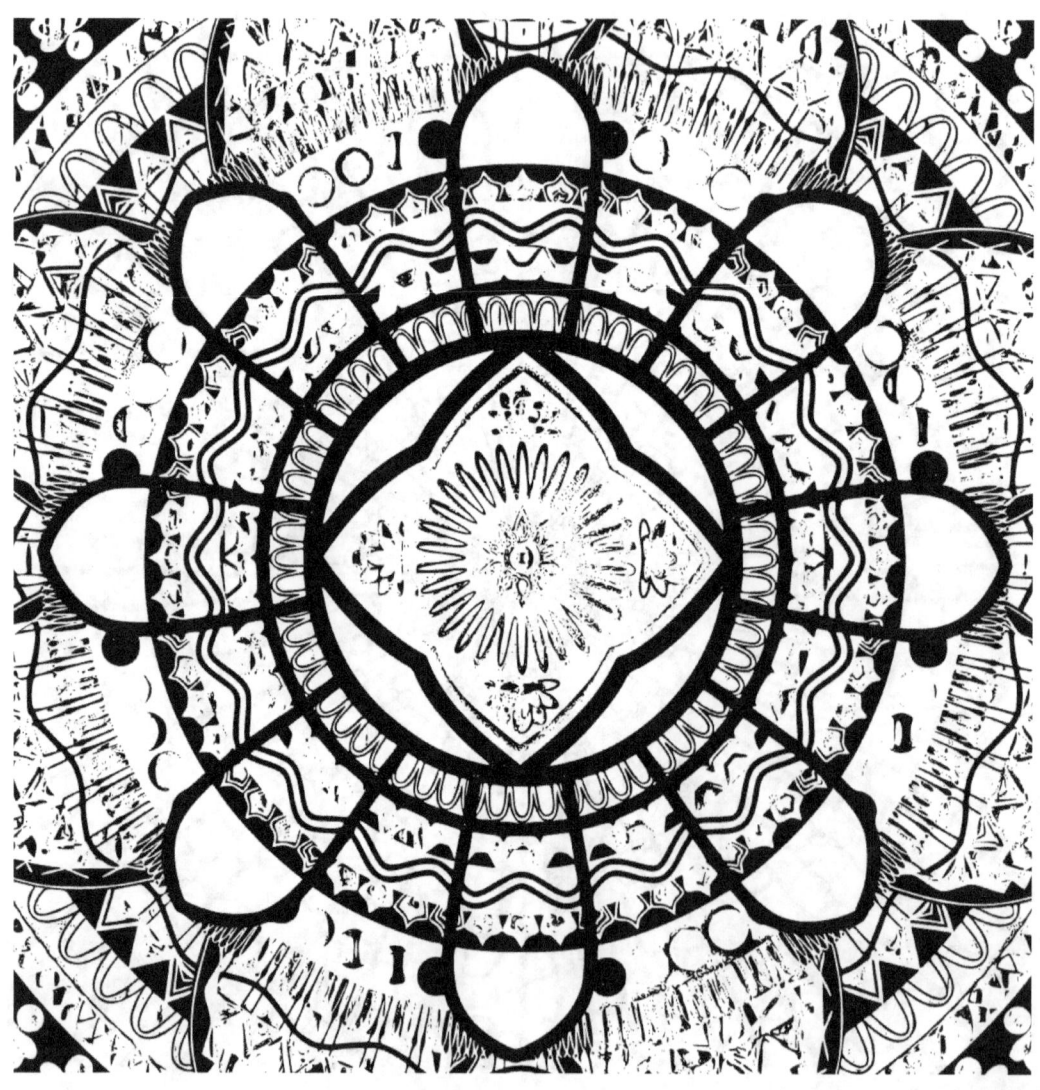

MANDALA

ART

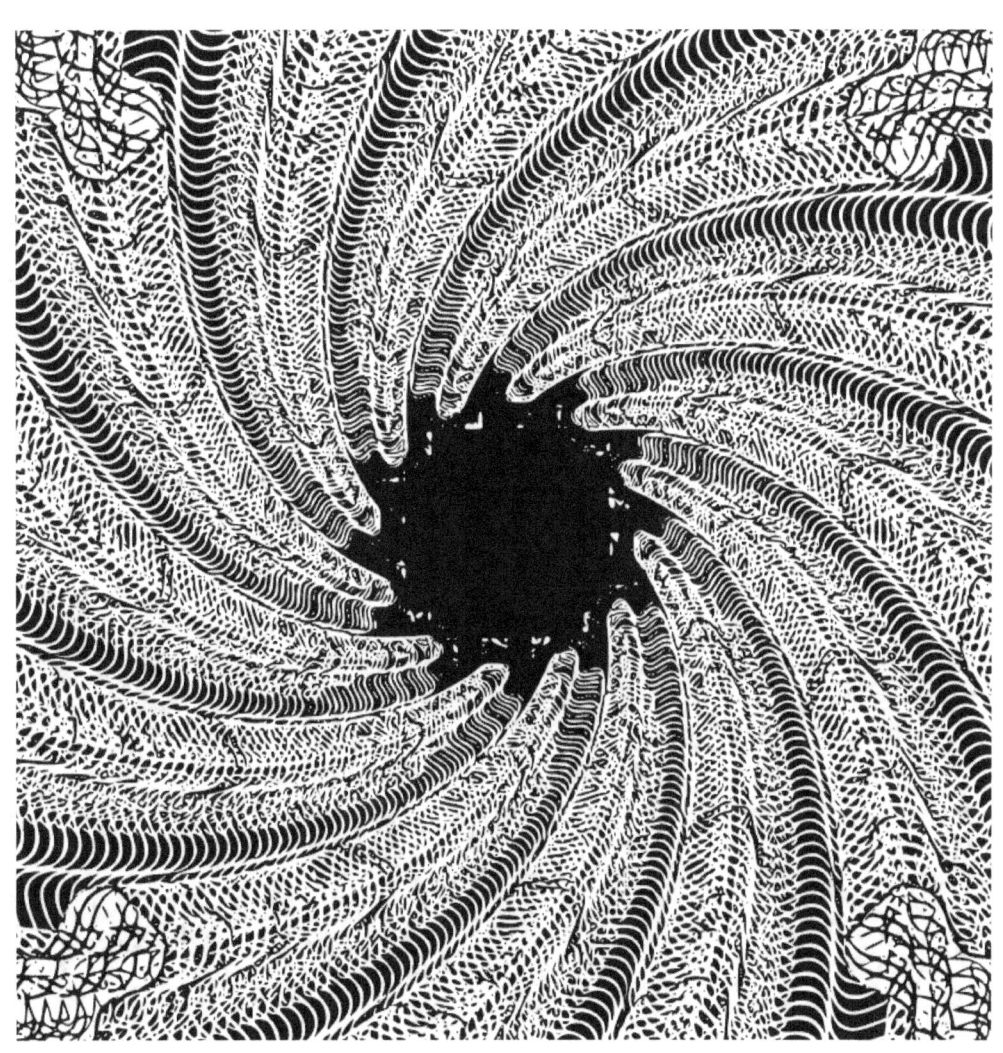

MANDALA
ART

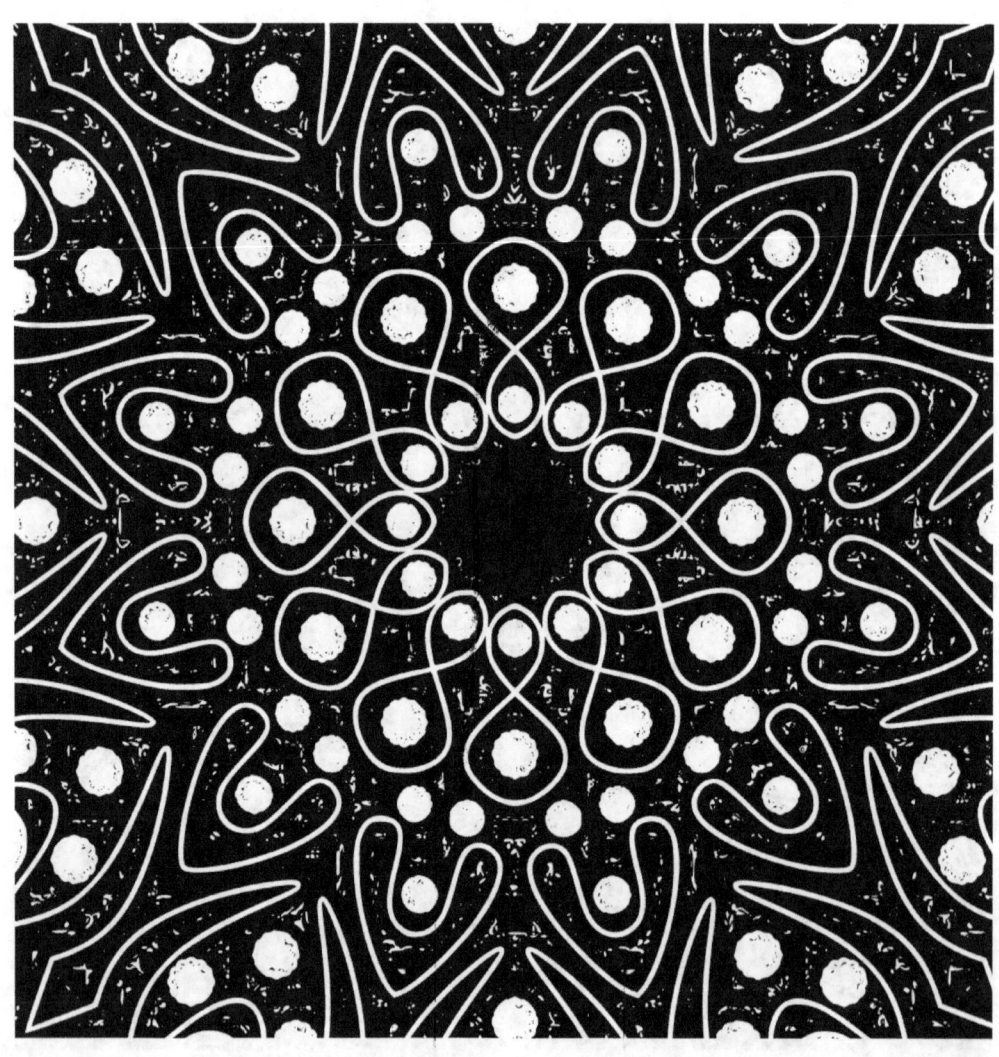

MANDALA

ART

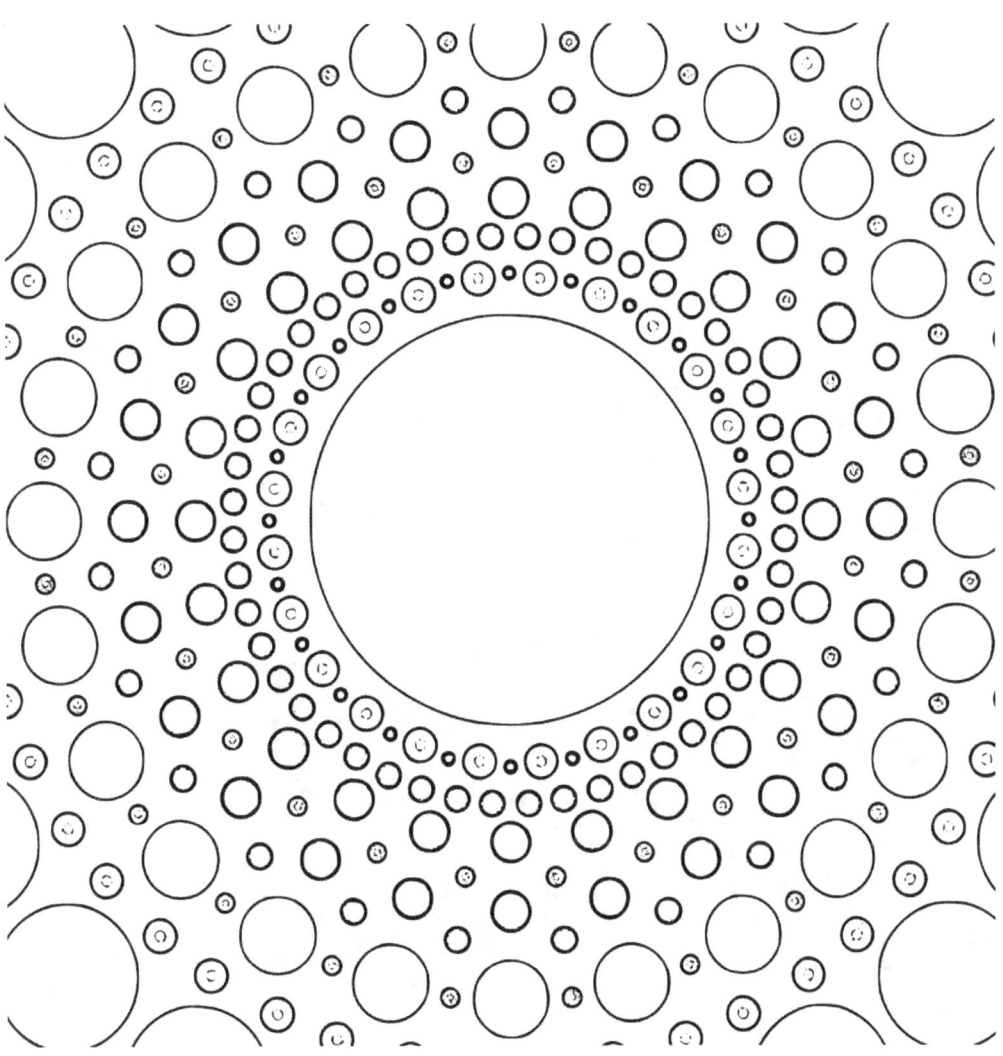

MANDALA
ART

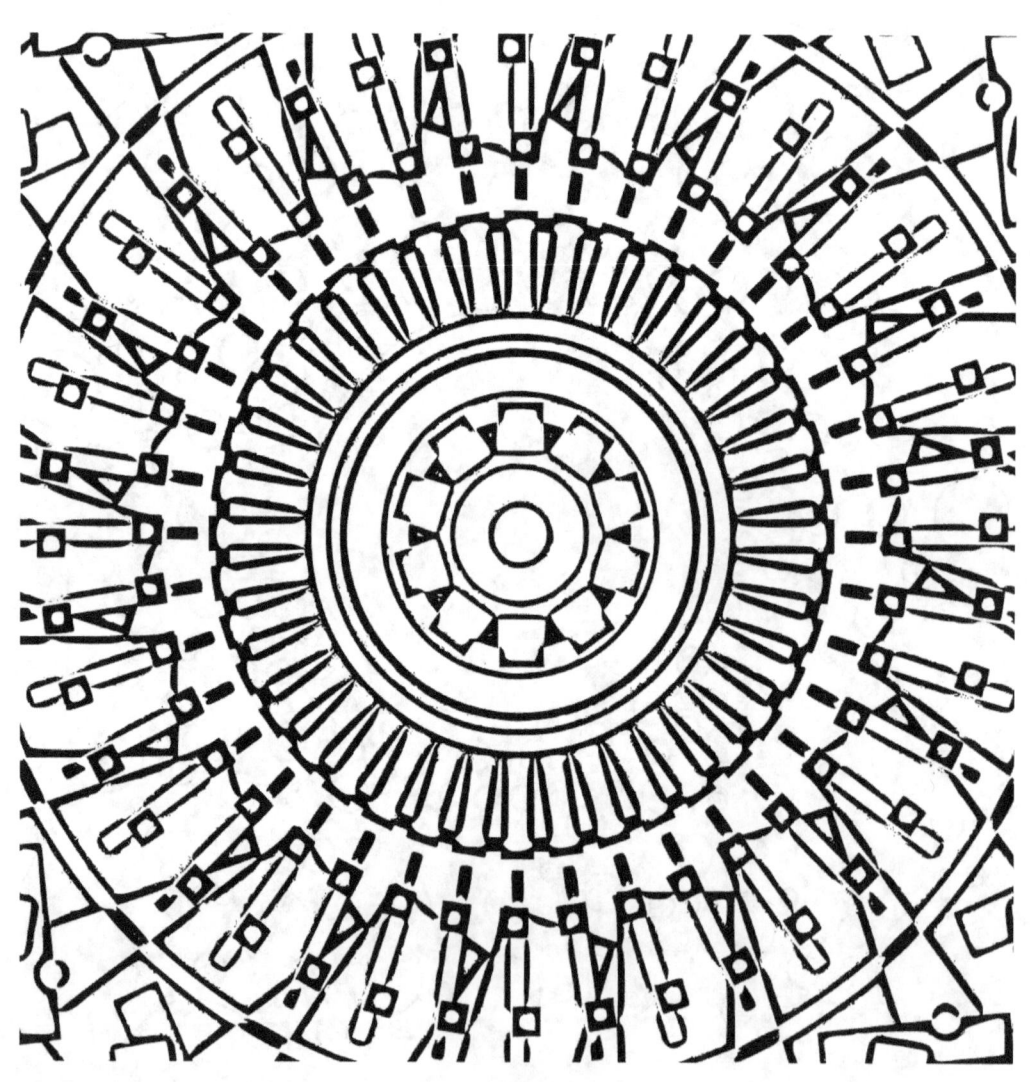

MANDALA
ART

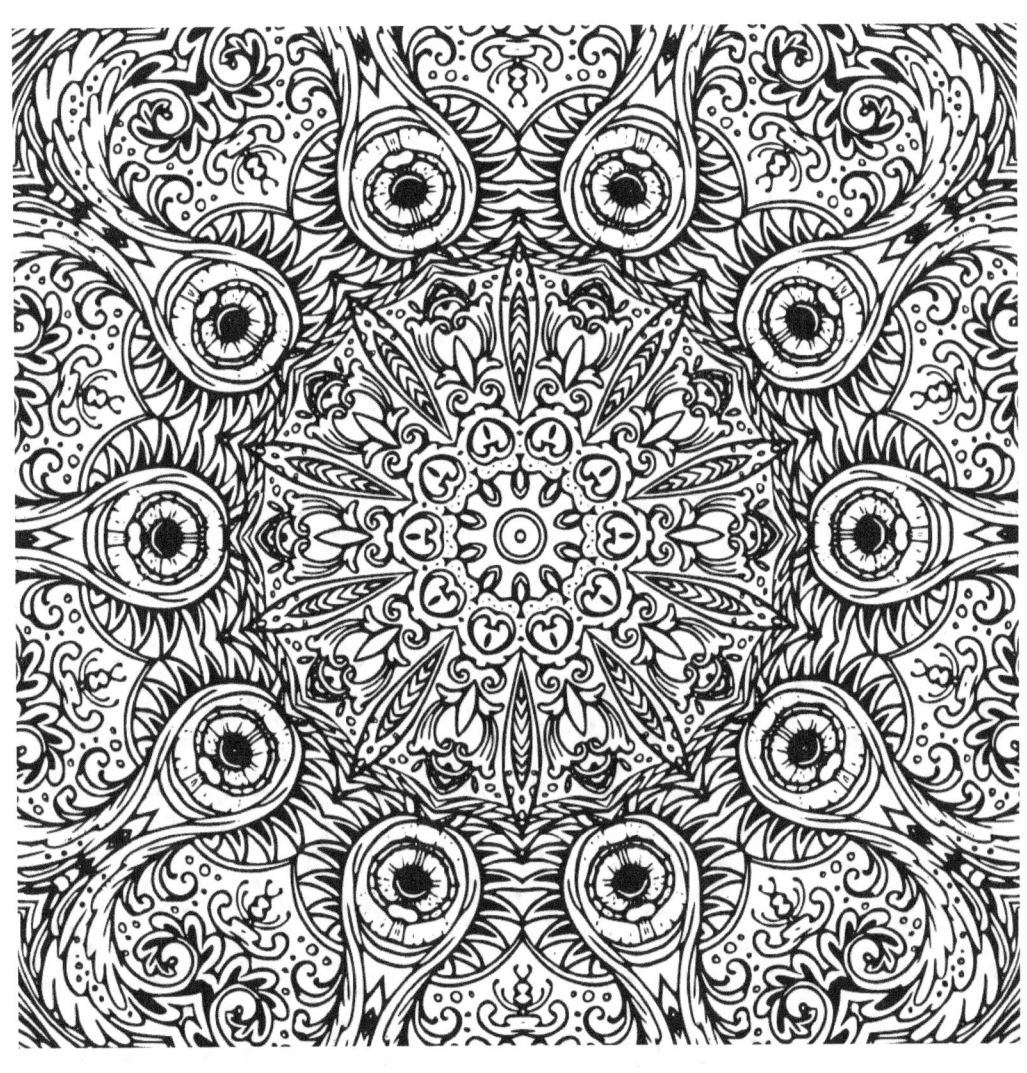

MANDALA
ART

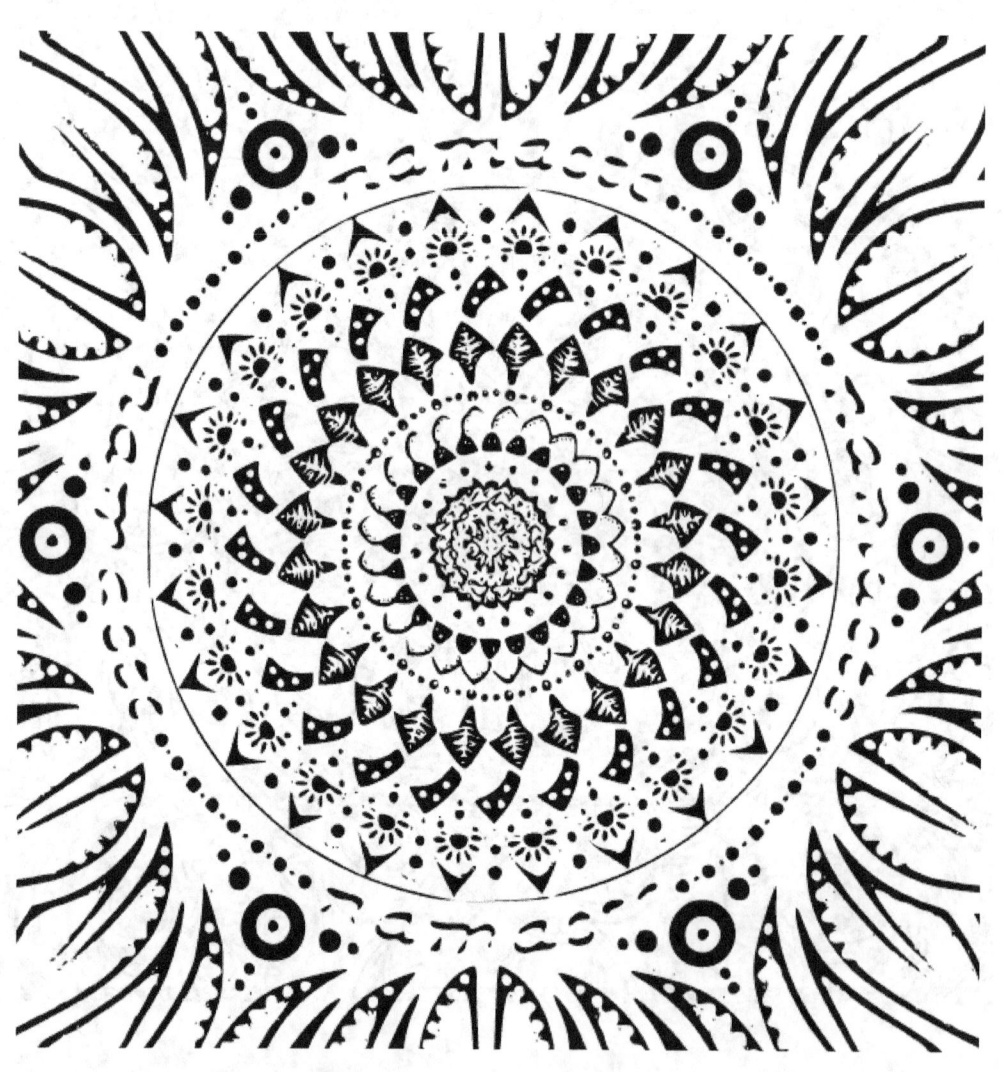

MANDALA
ART

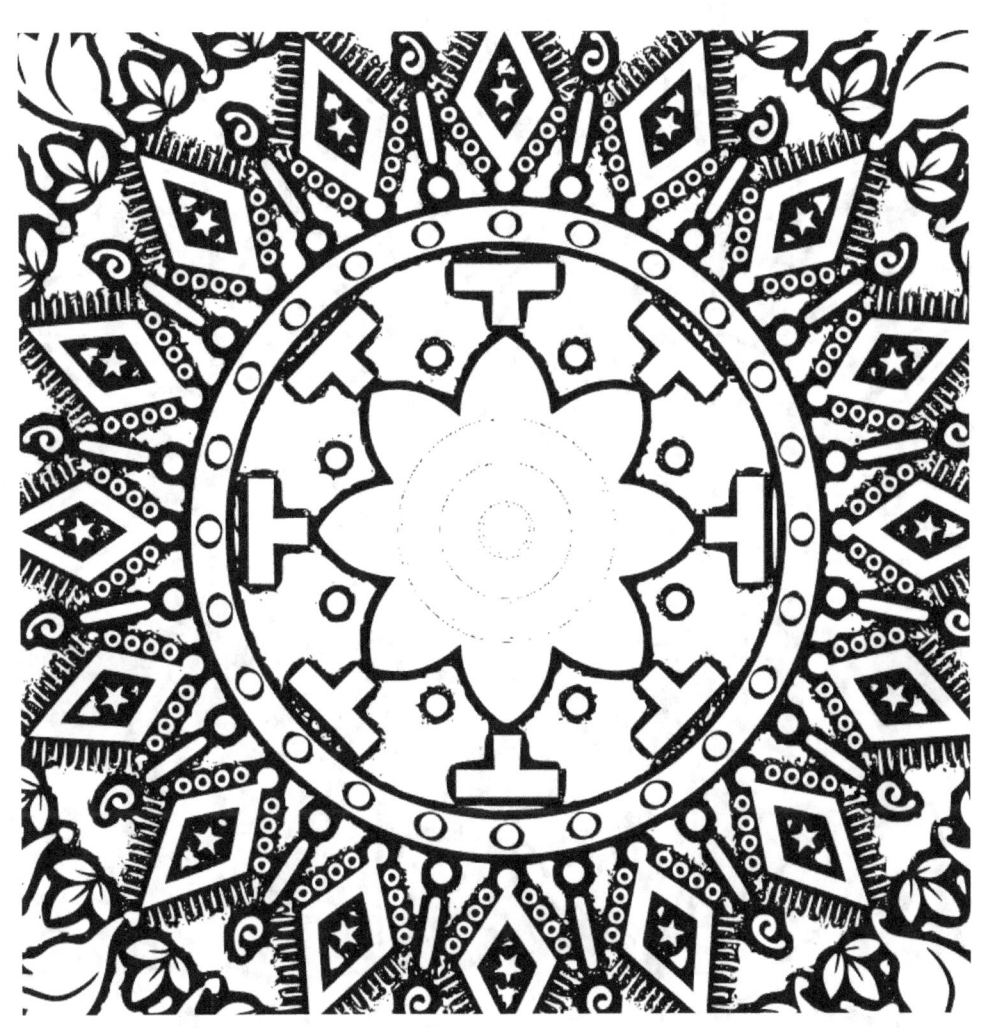

MANDALA

ART

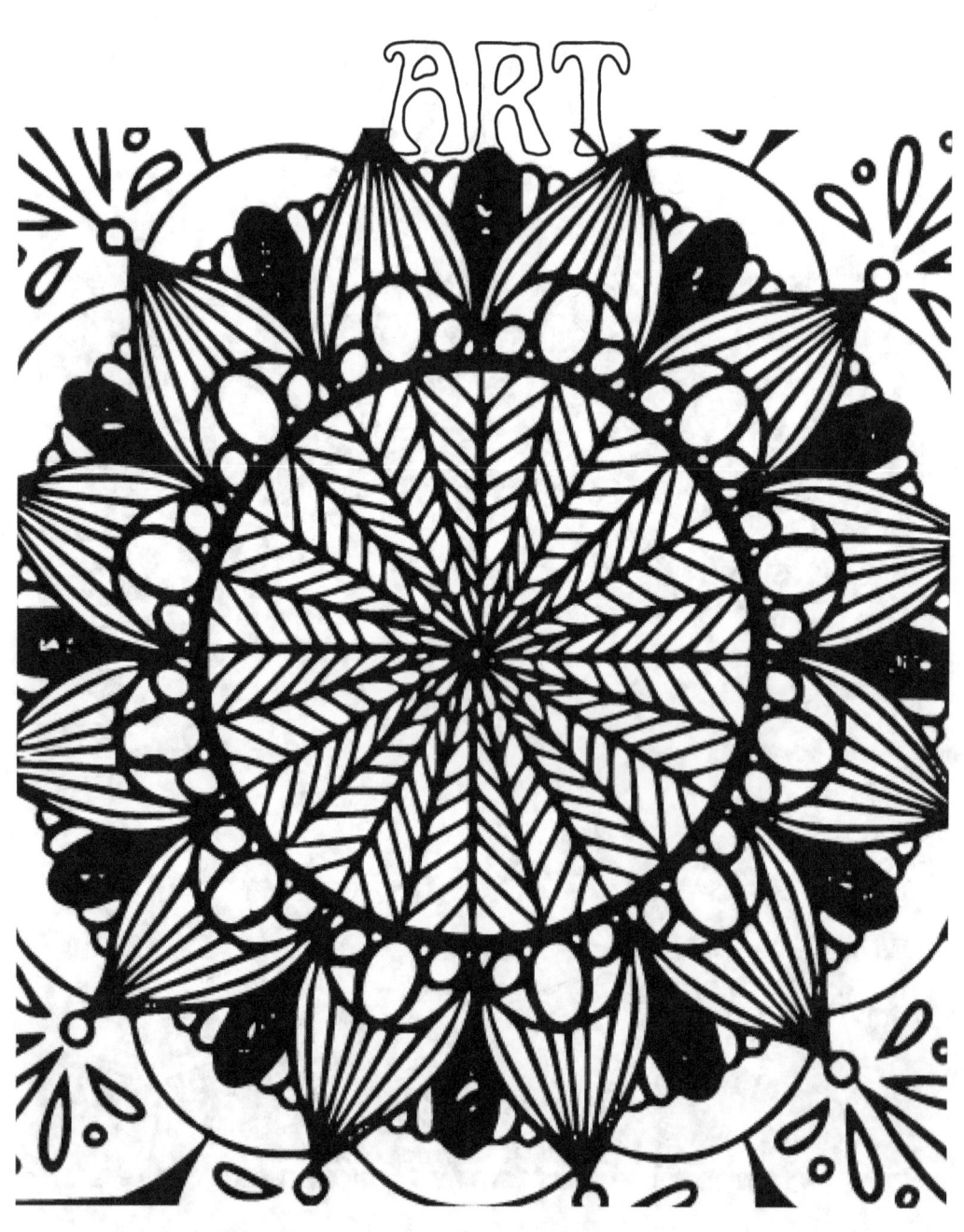

MANDALA

ART

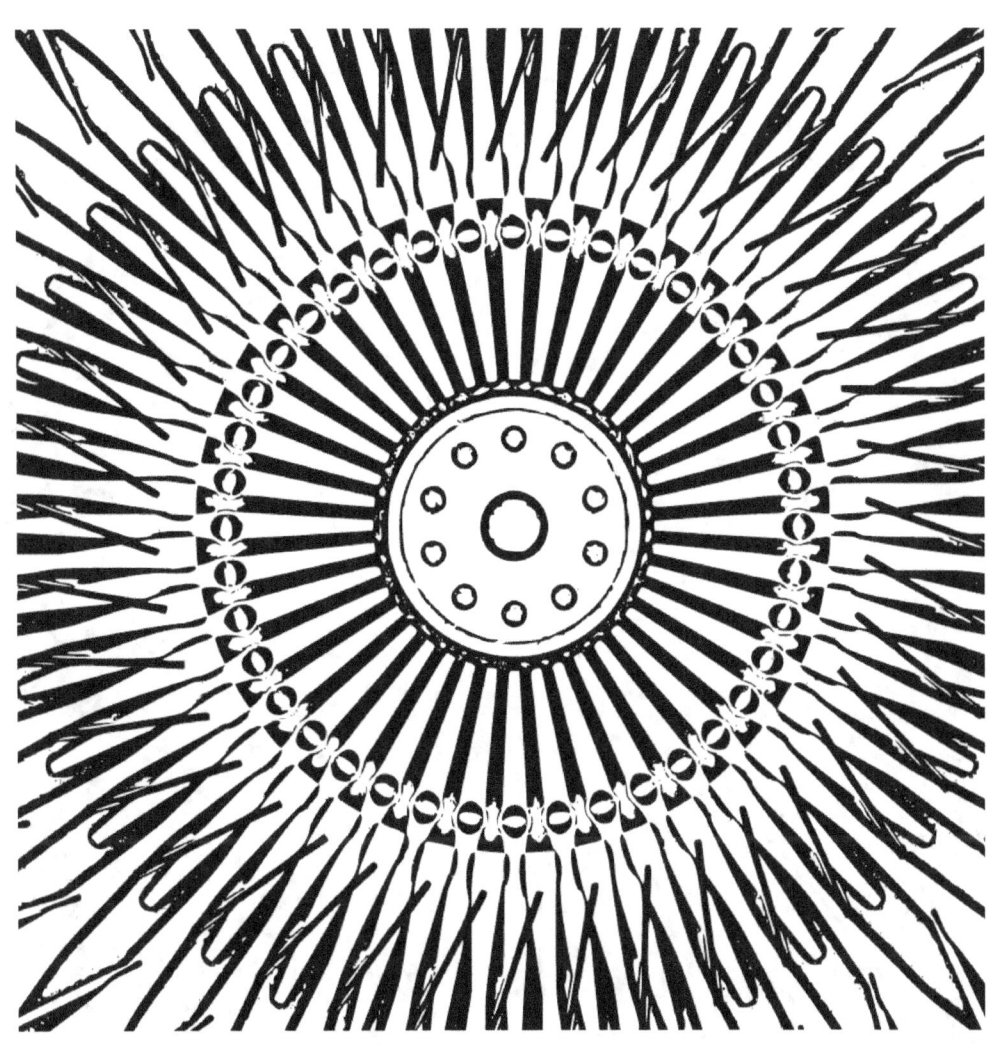

MANDALA

ART

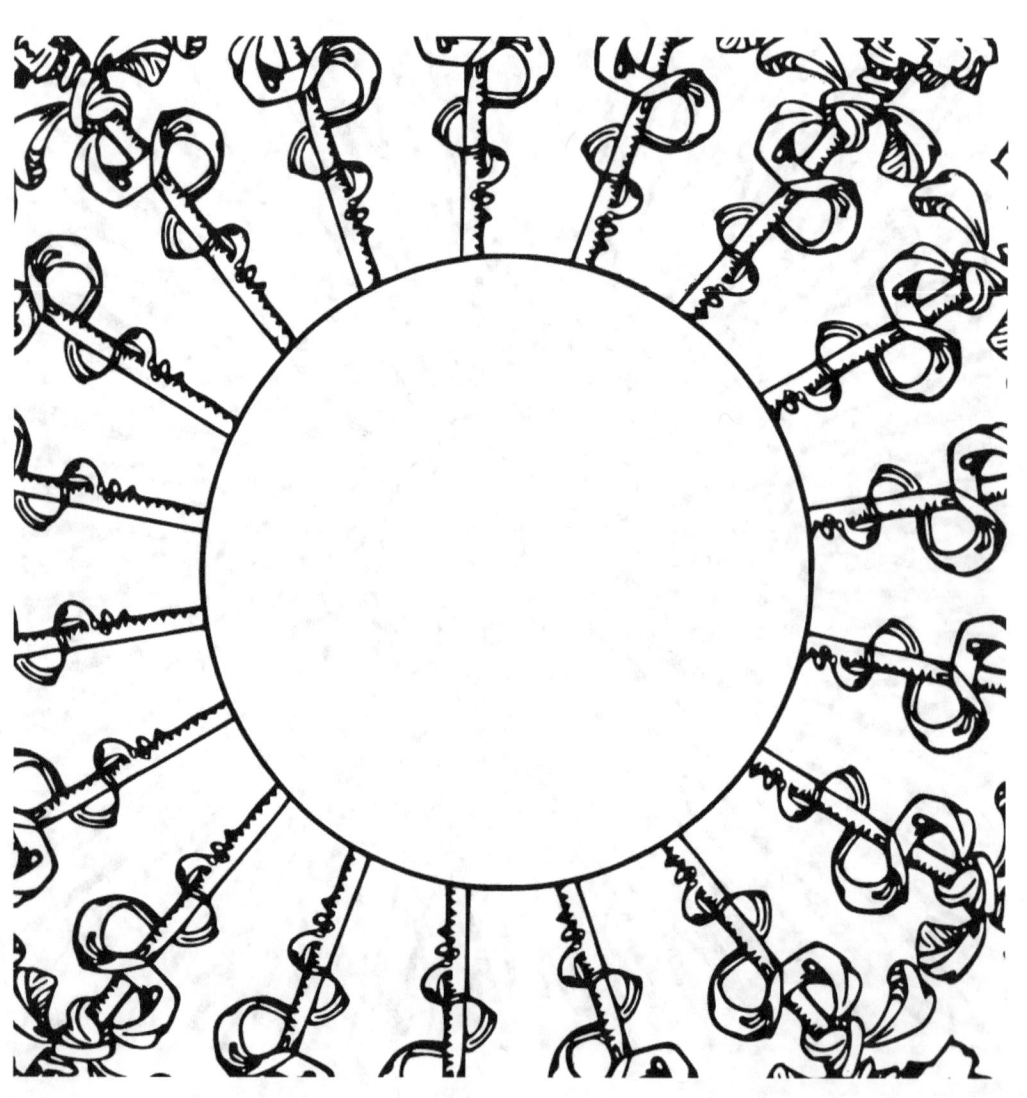

MANDALA

ART

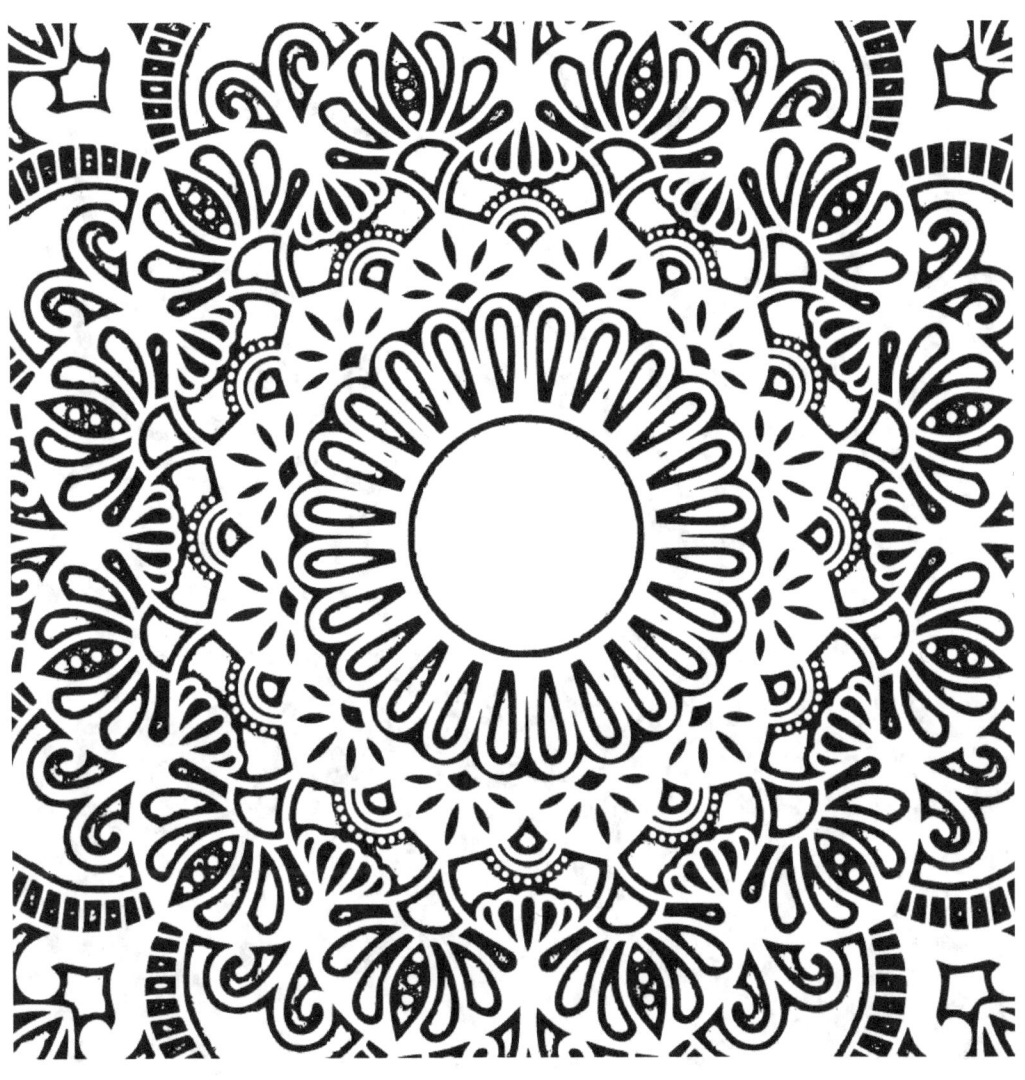

MANDALA

ART

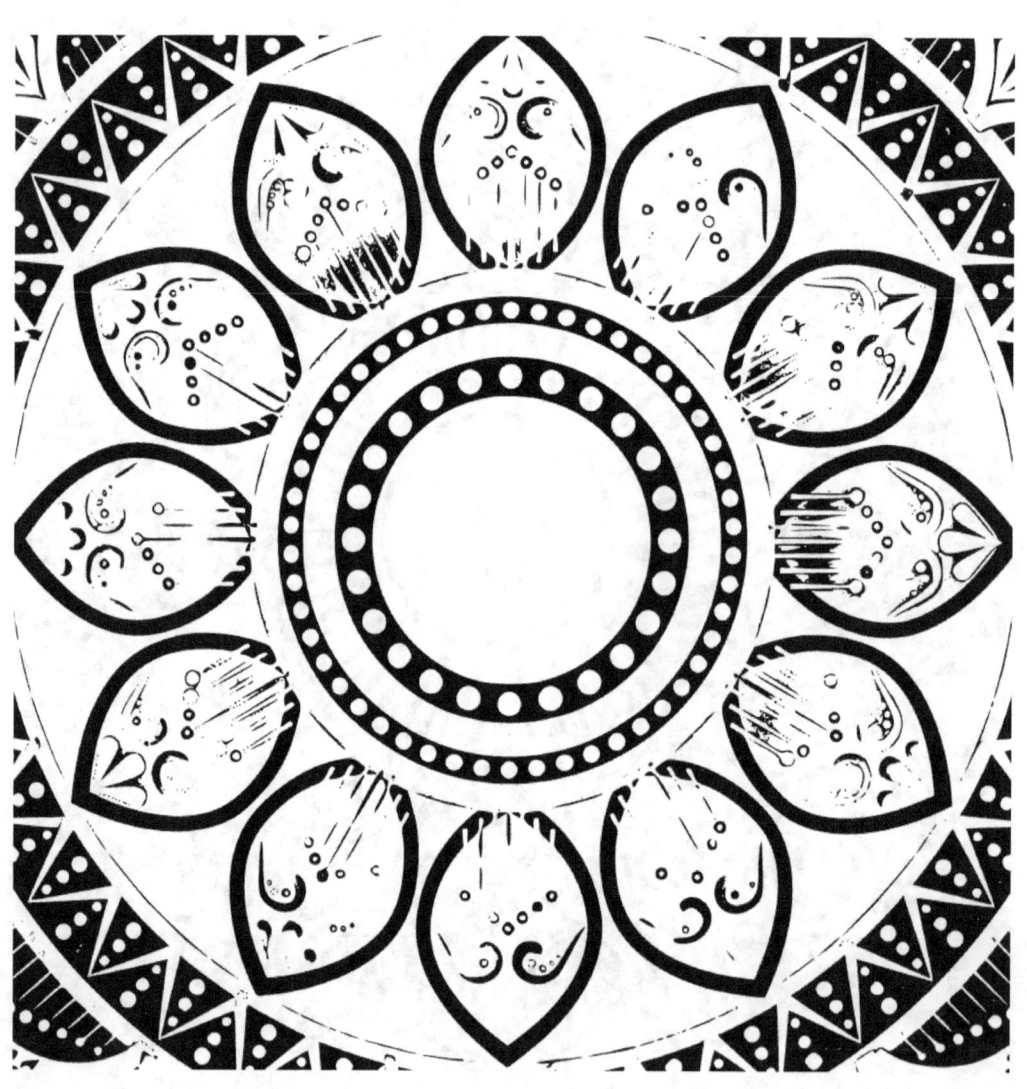

MANDALA
ART

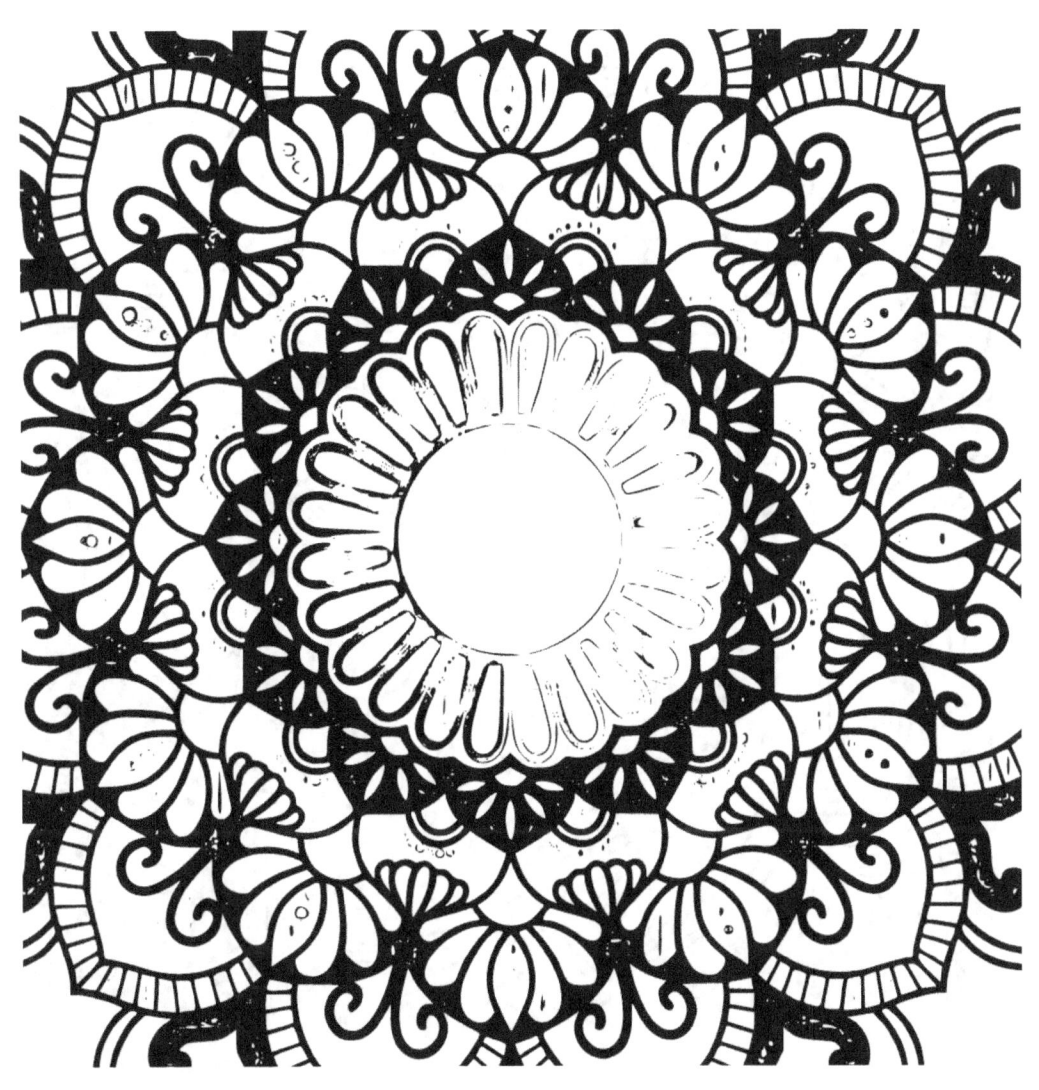

MANDALA
ART

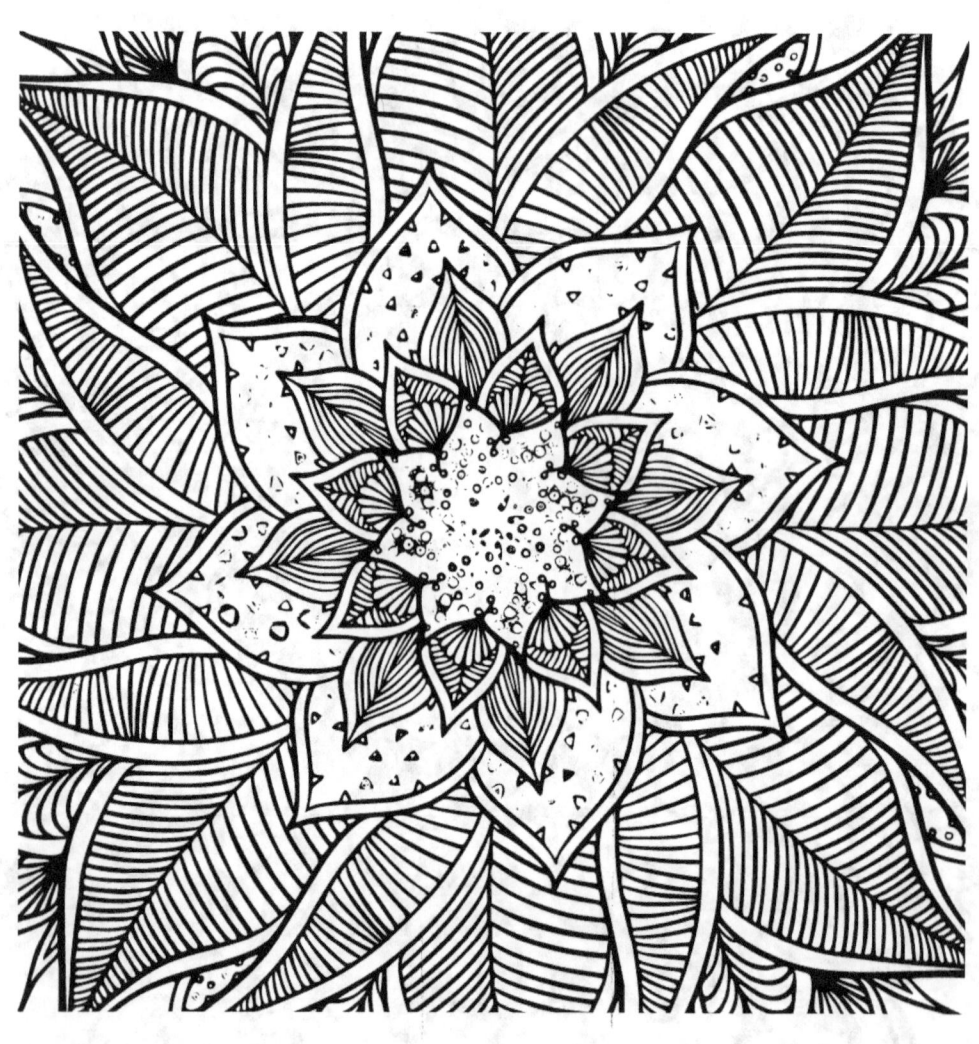

MANDALA
ART

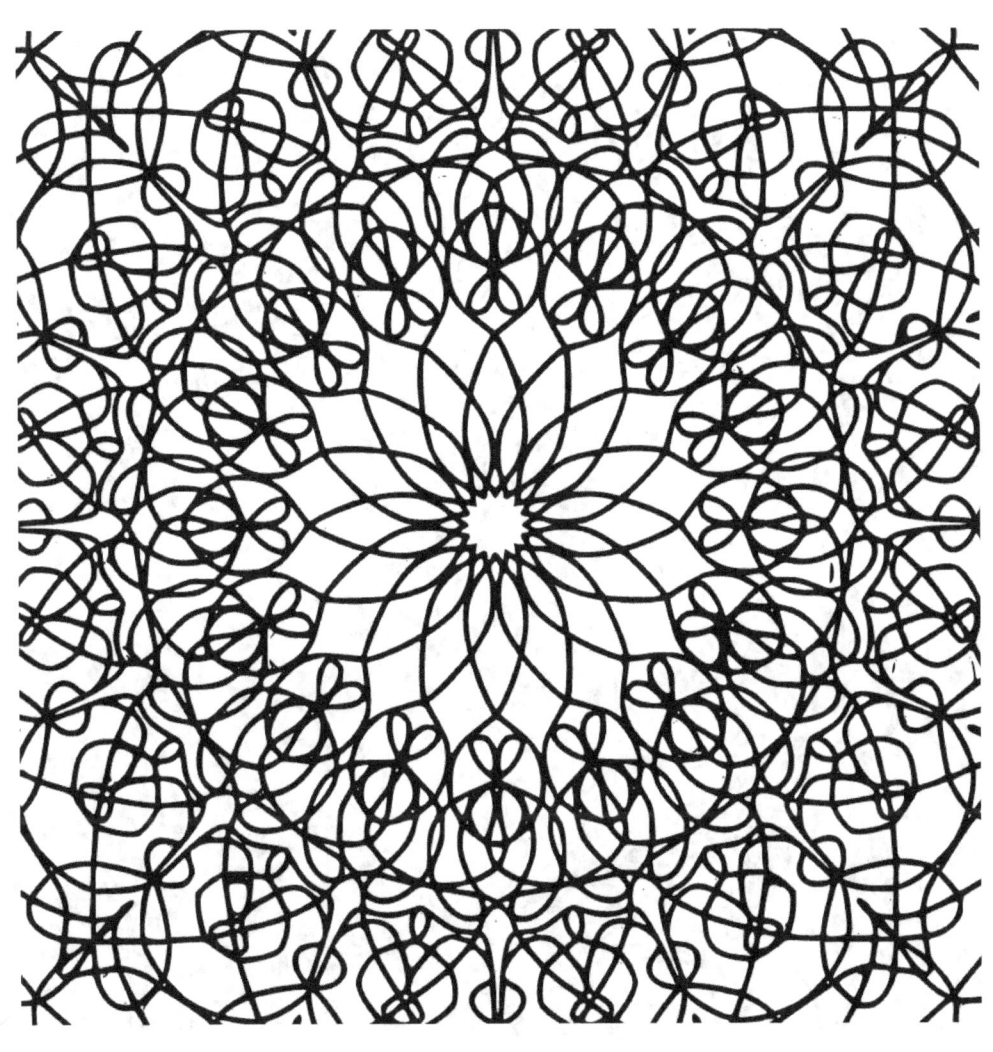

MANDALA
ART

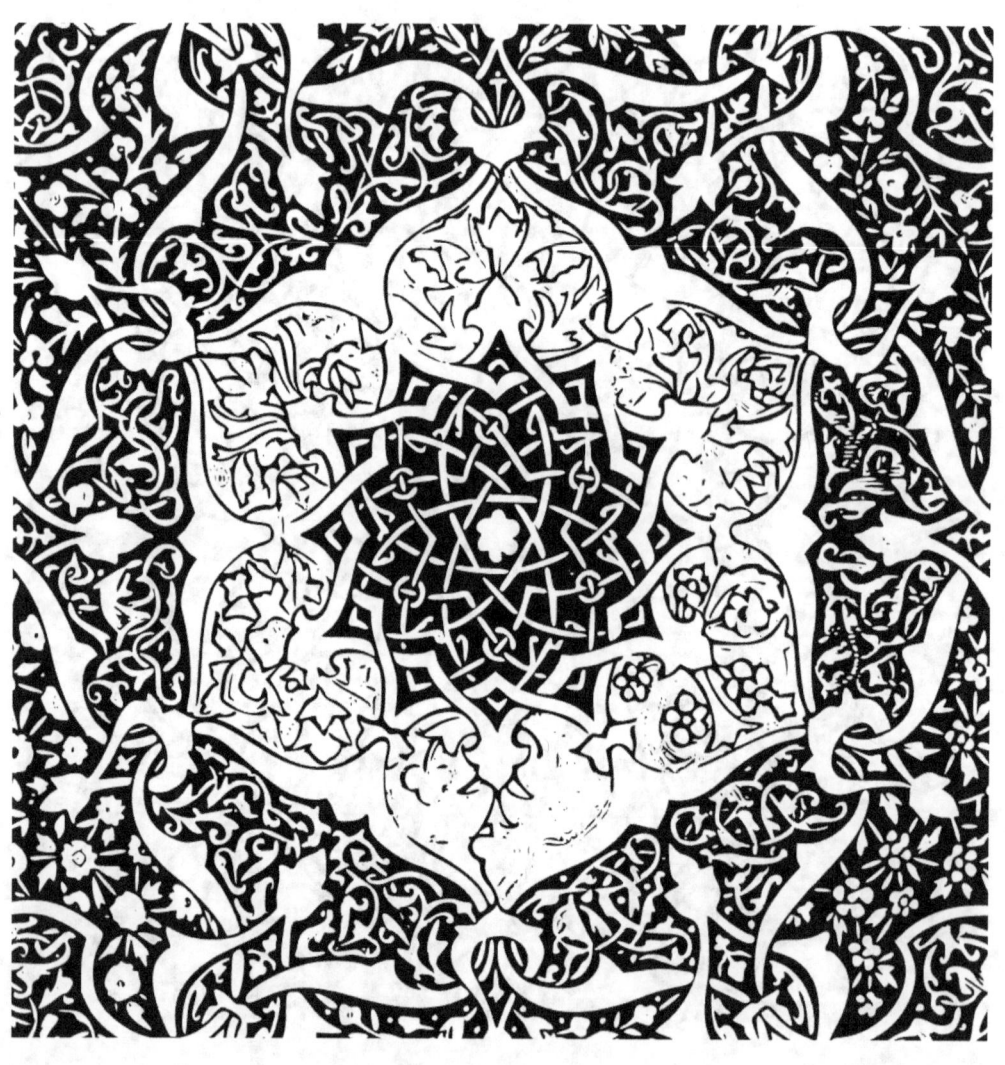

MANDALA

ART

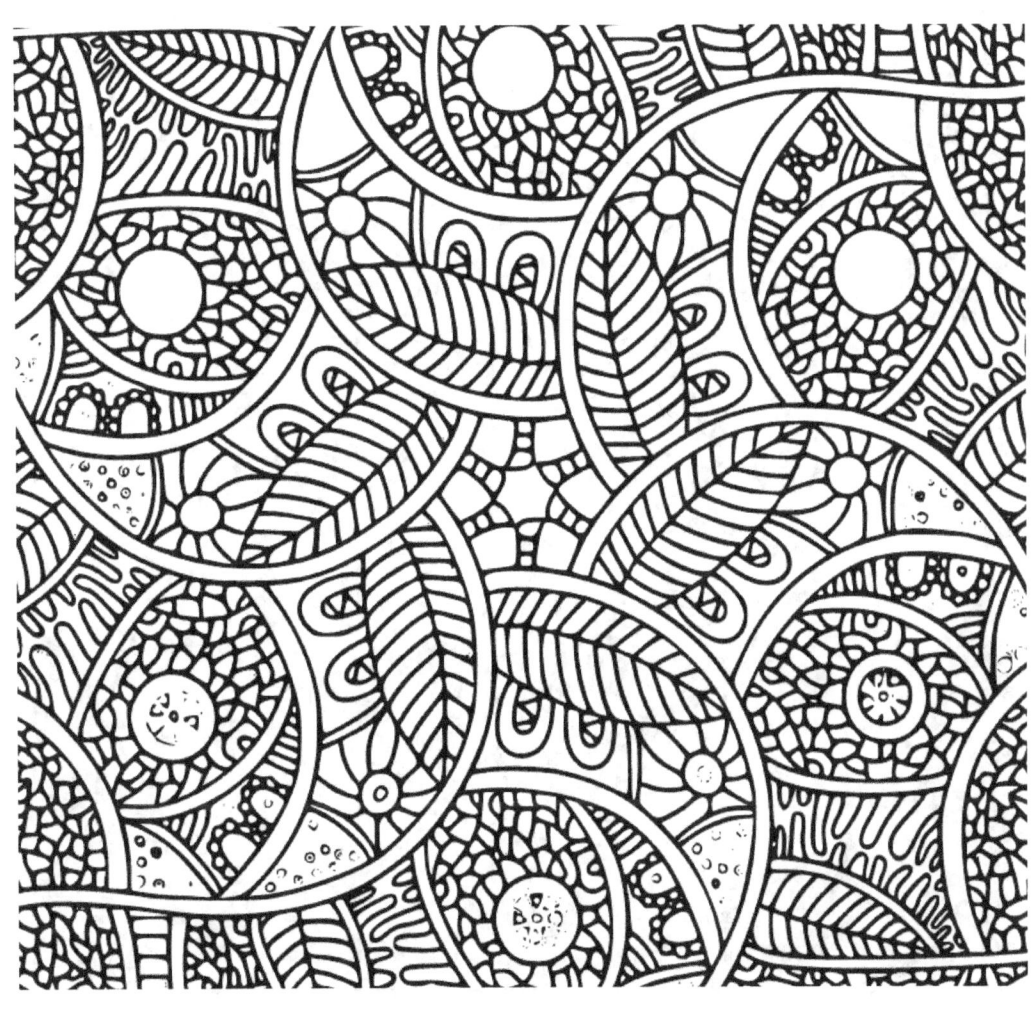

MANDALA
ART

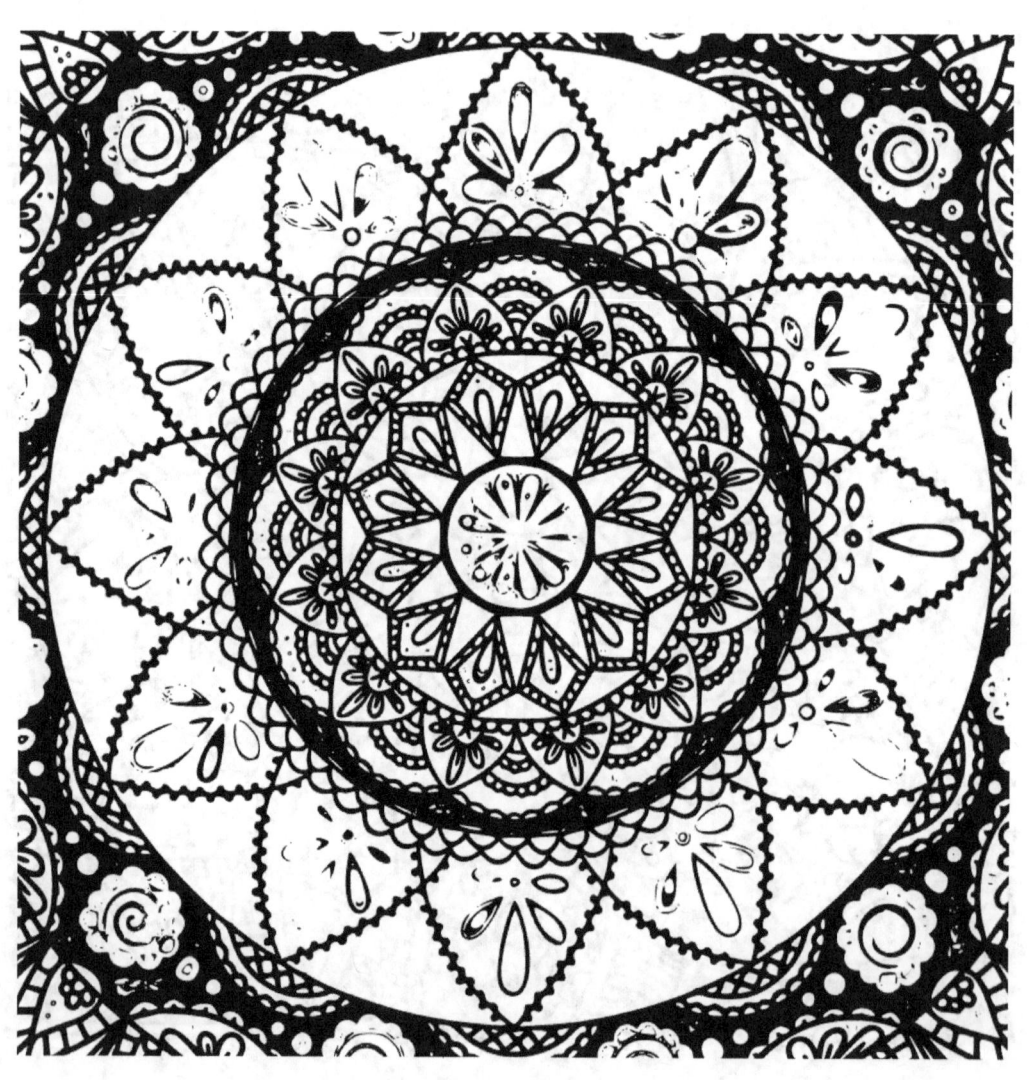

MANDALA
ART

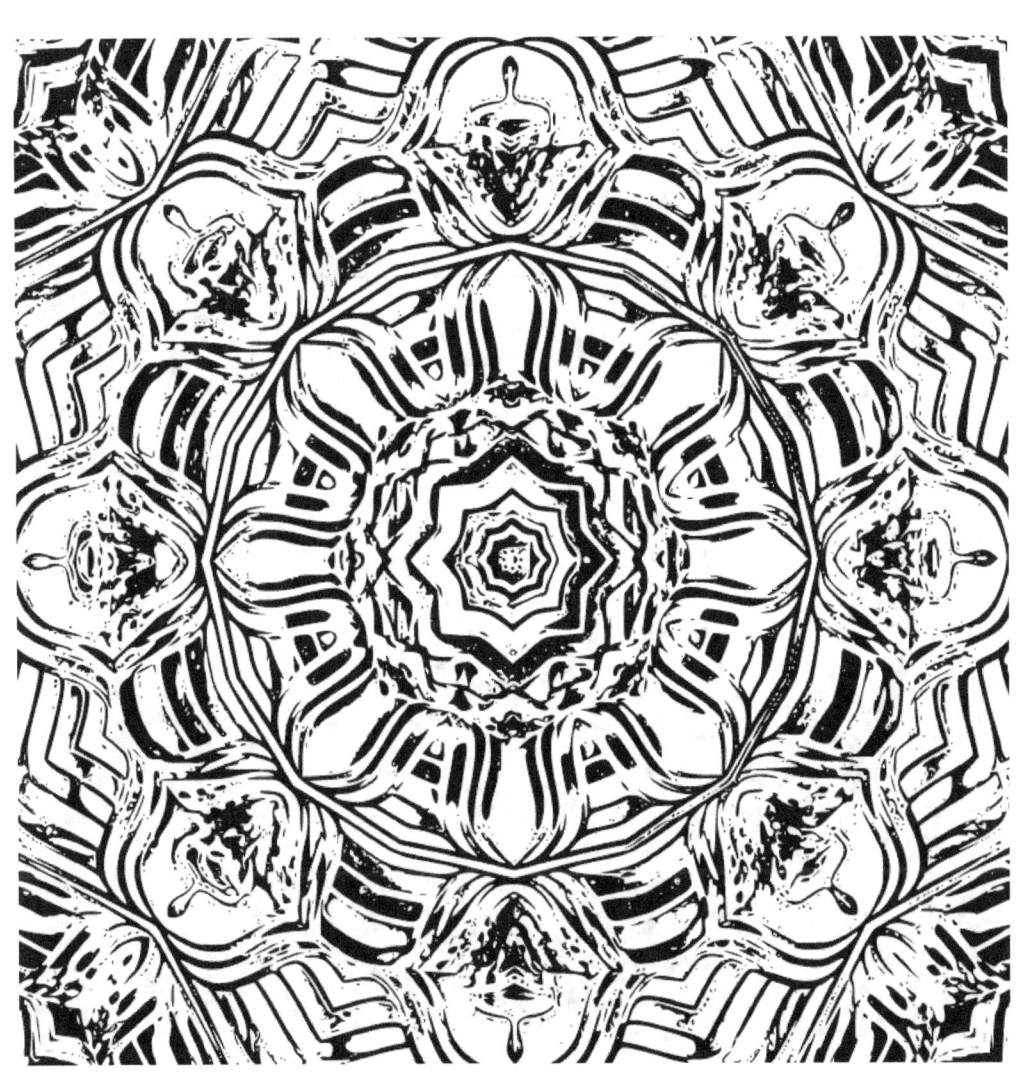

MANDALA
ART

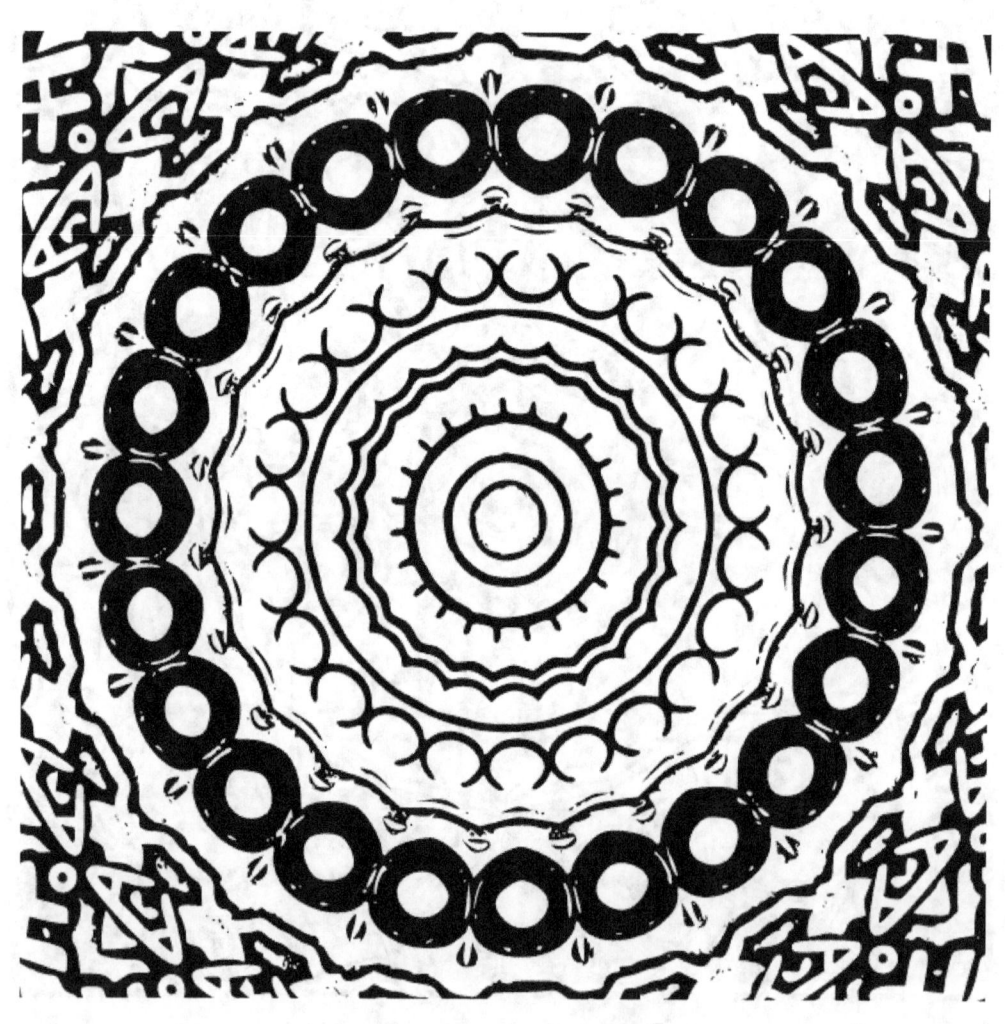

MANDALA

ART

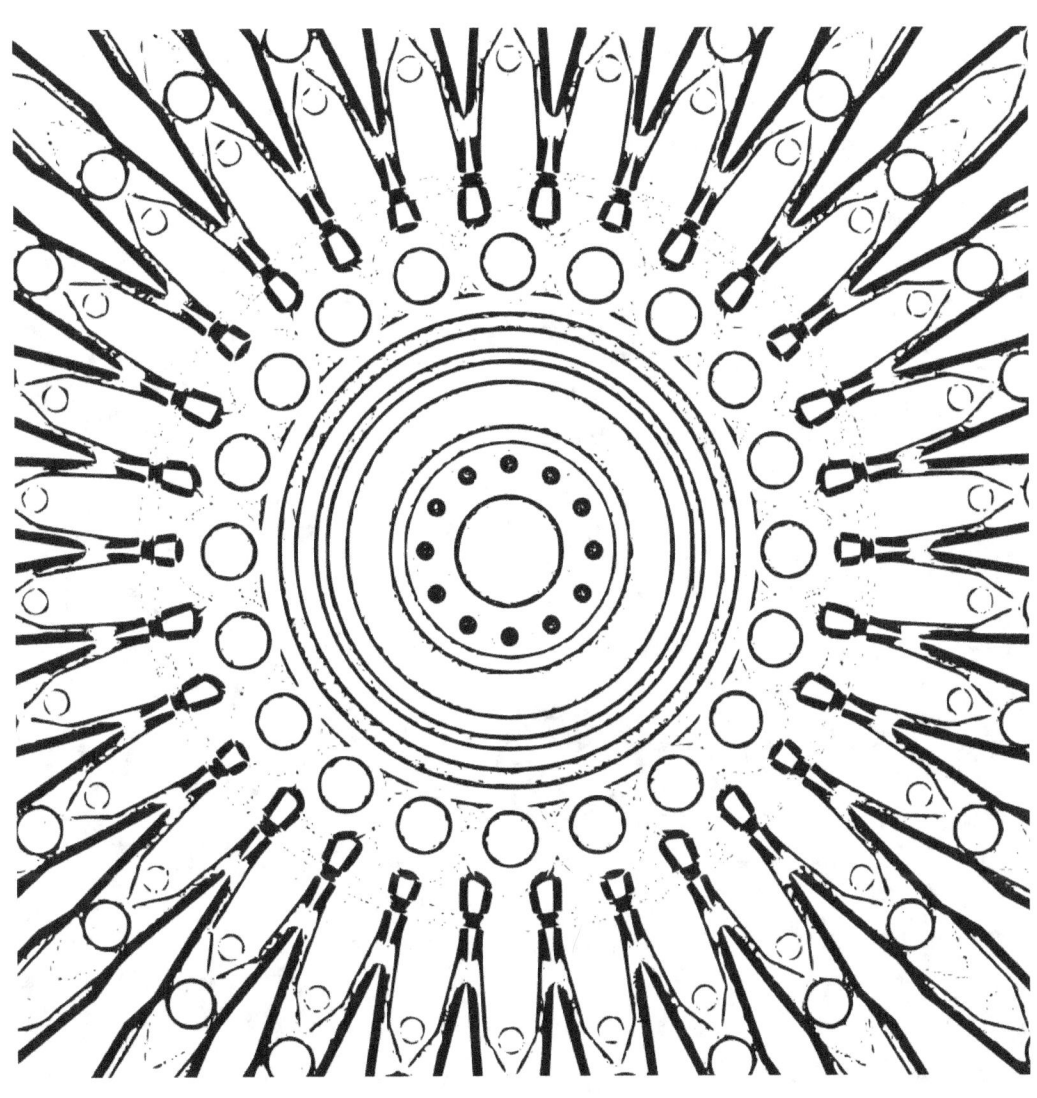

MANDALA
ART

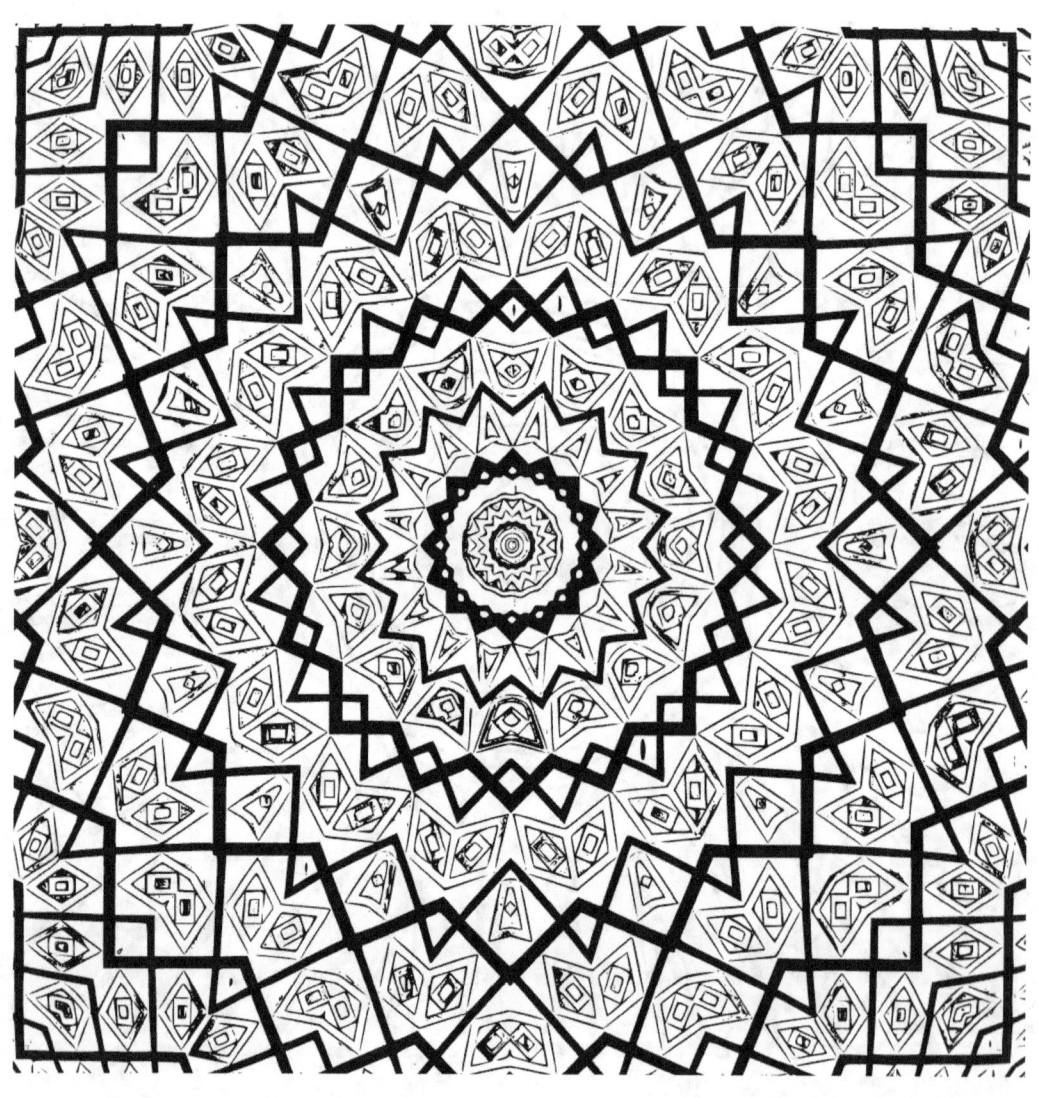

MANDALA

ART

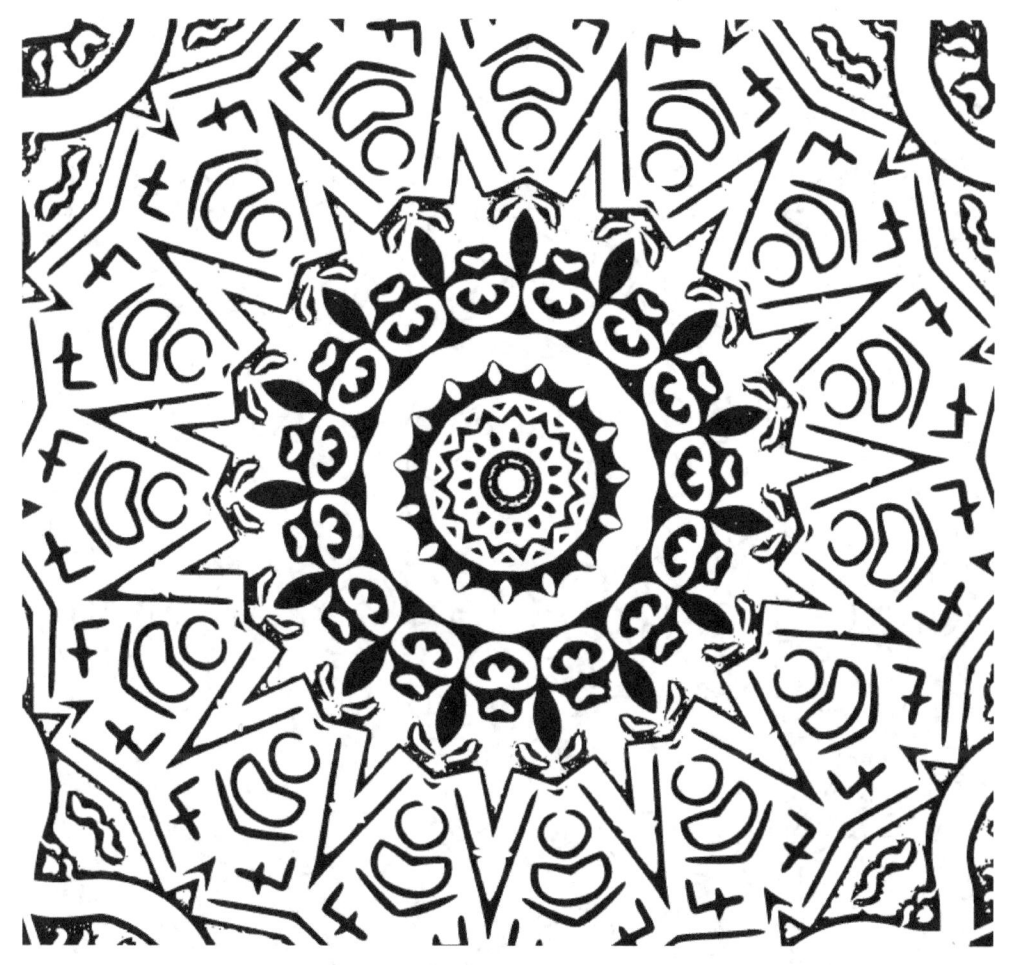

MANDALA
ART

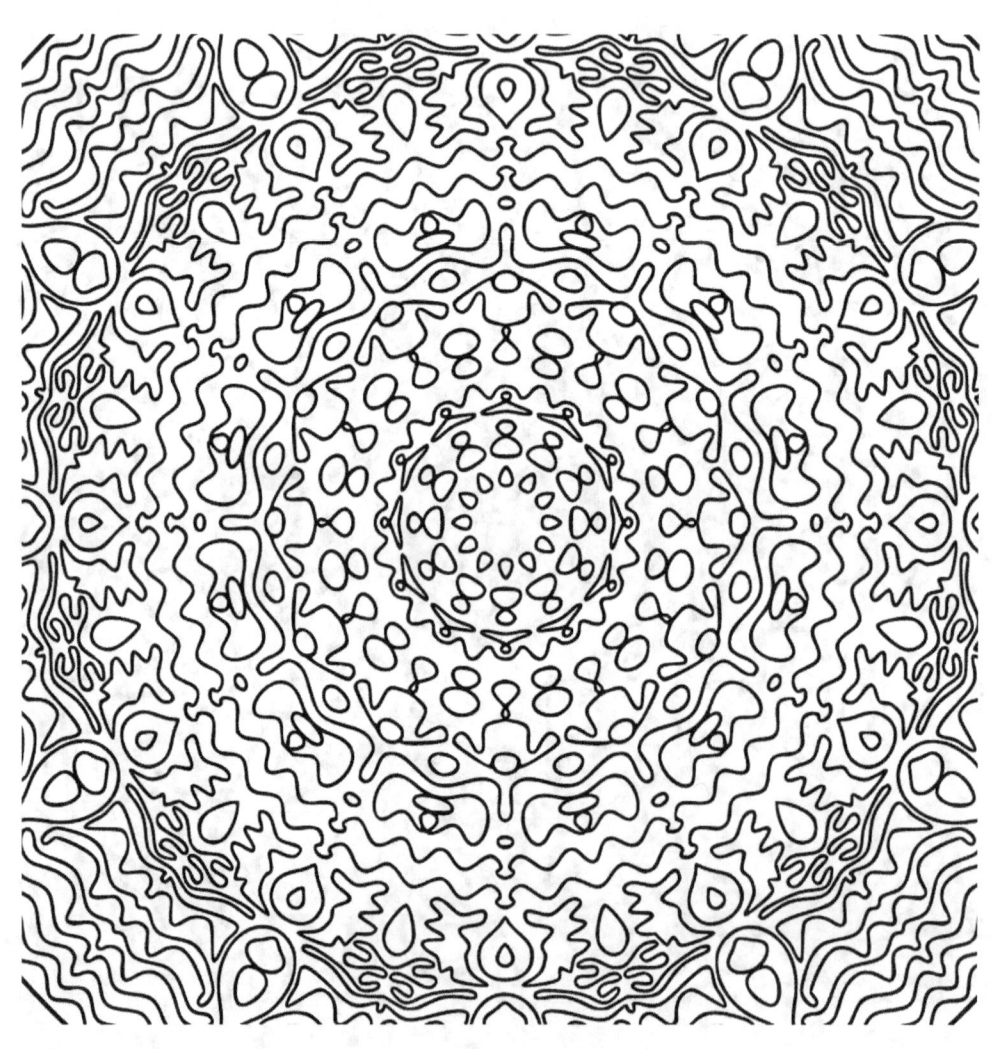

MANDALA

ART

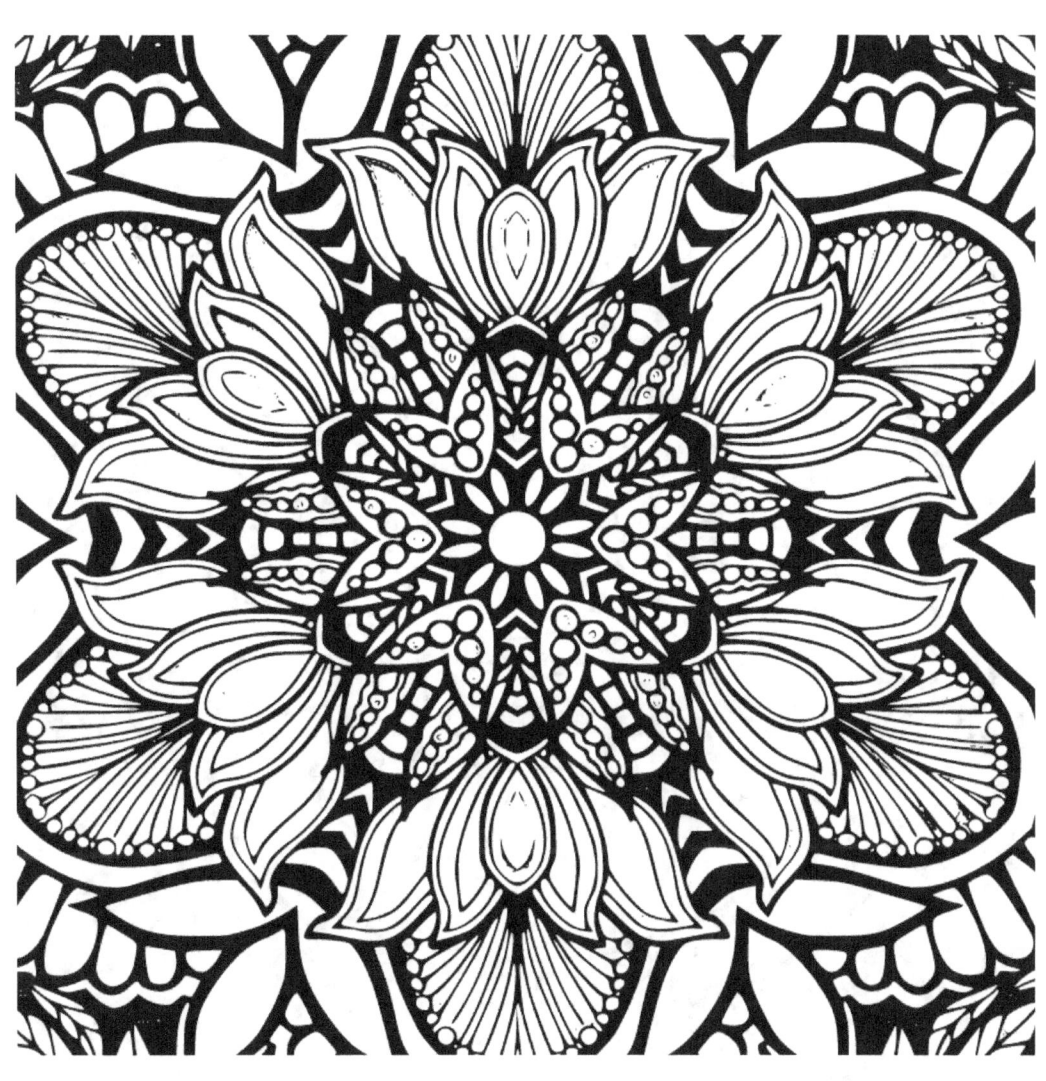

MANDALA
ART

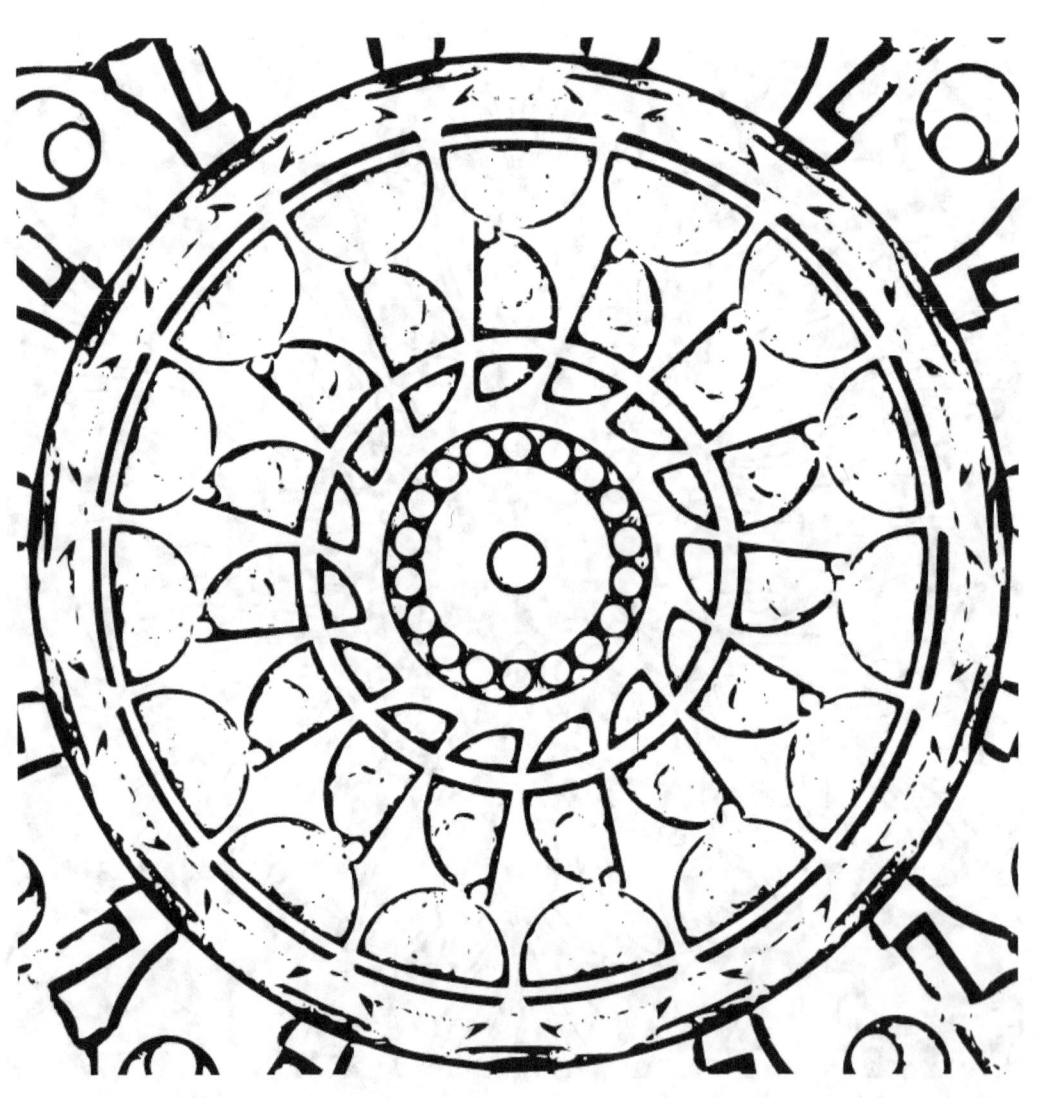

MANDALA
ART

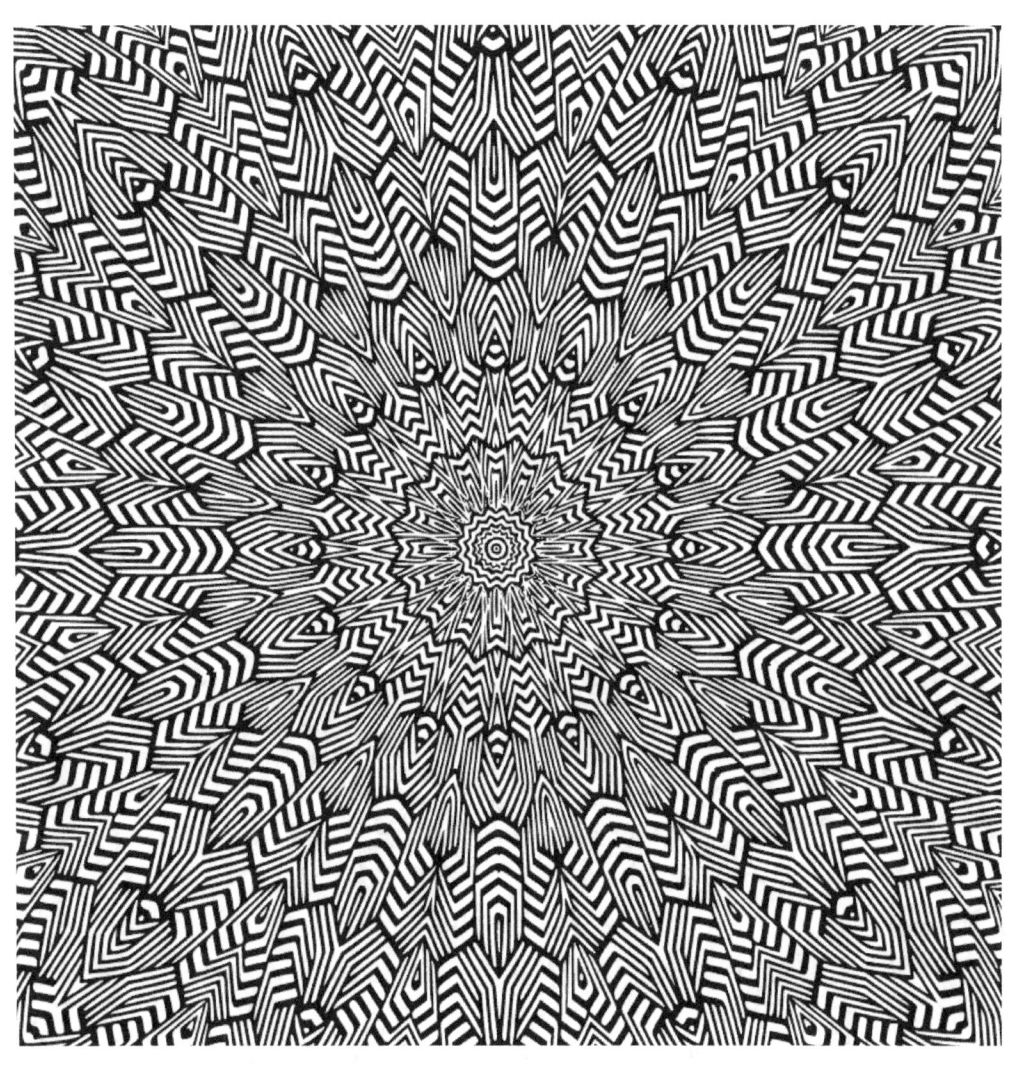

MANDALA
ART

MANDALA

ART

MANDALA
ART

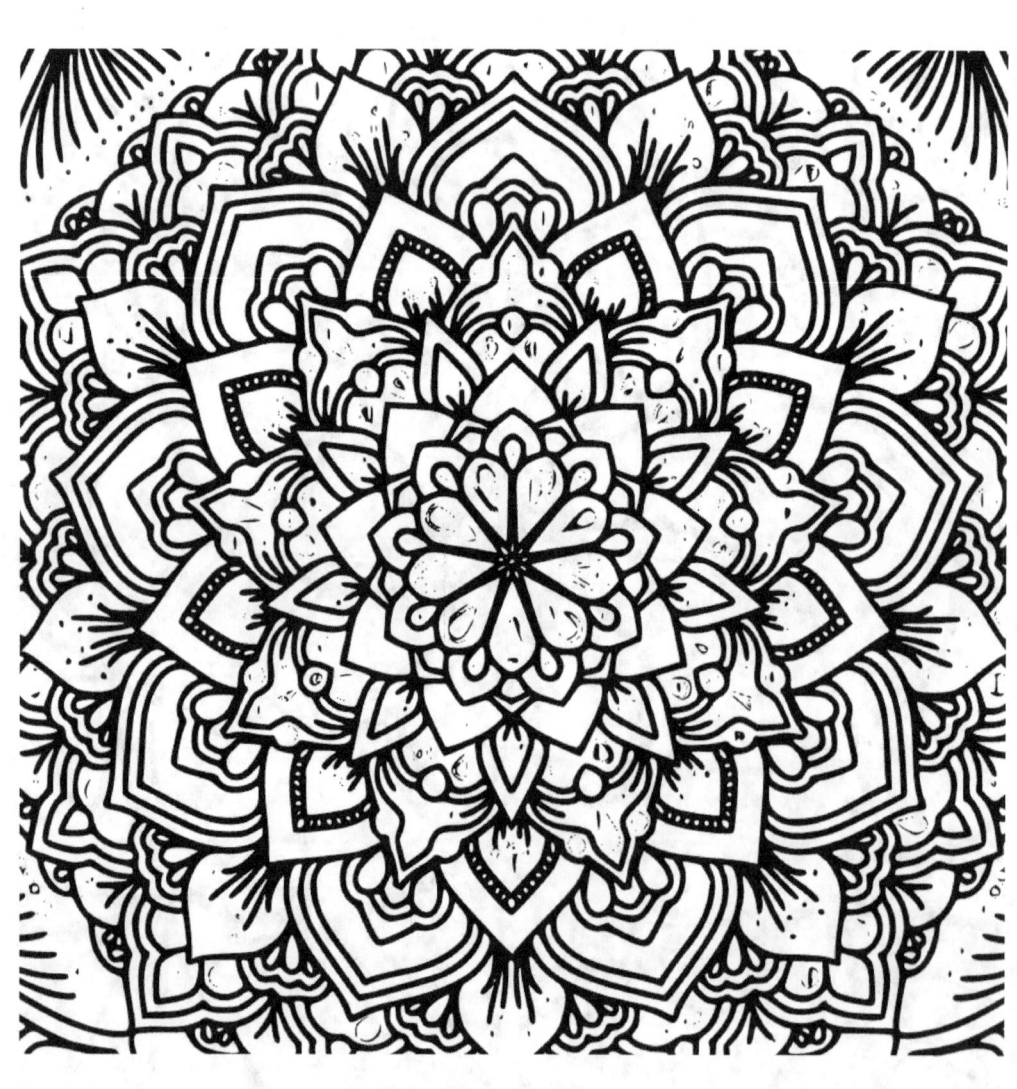

MANDALA
ART

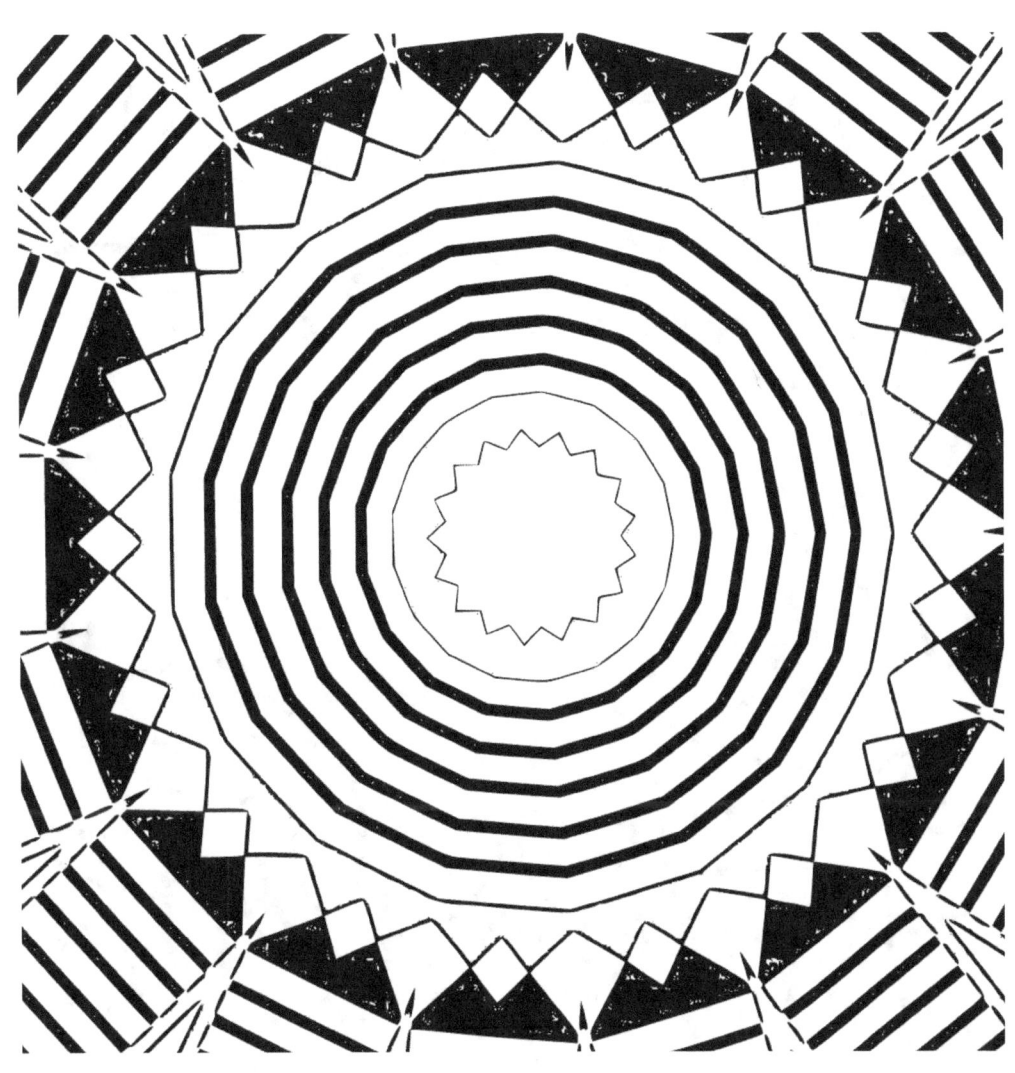

MANDALA
ART

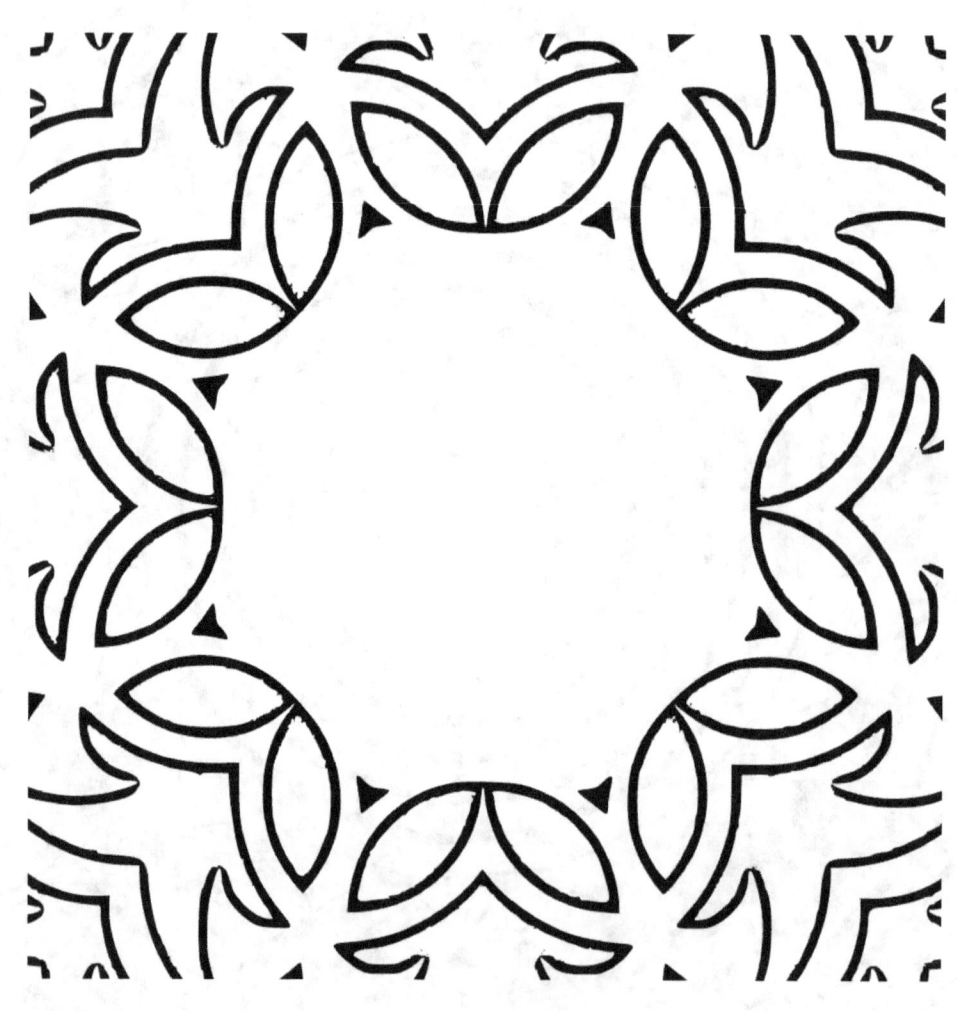

MANDALA
ART

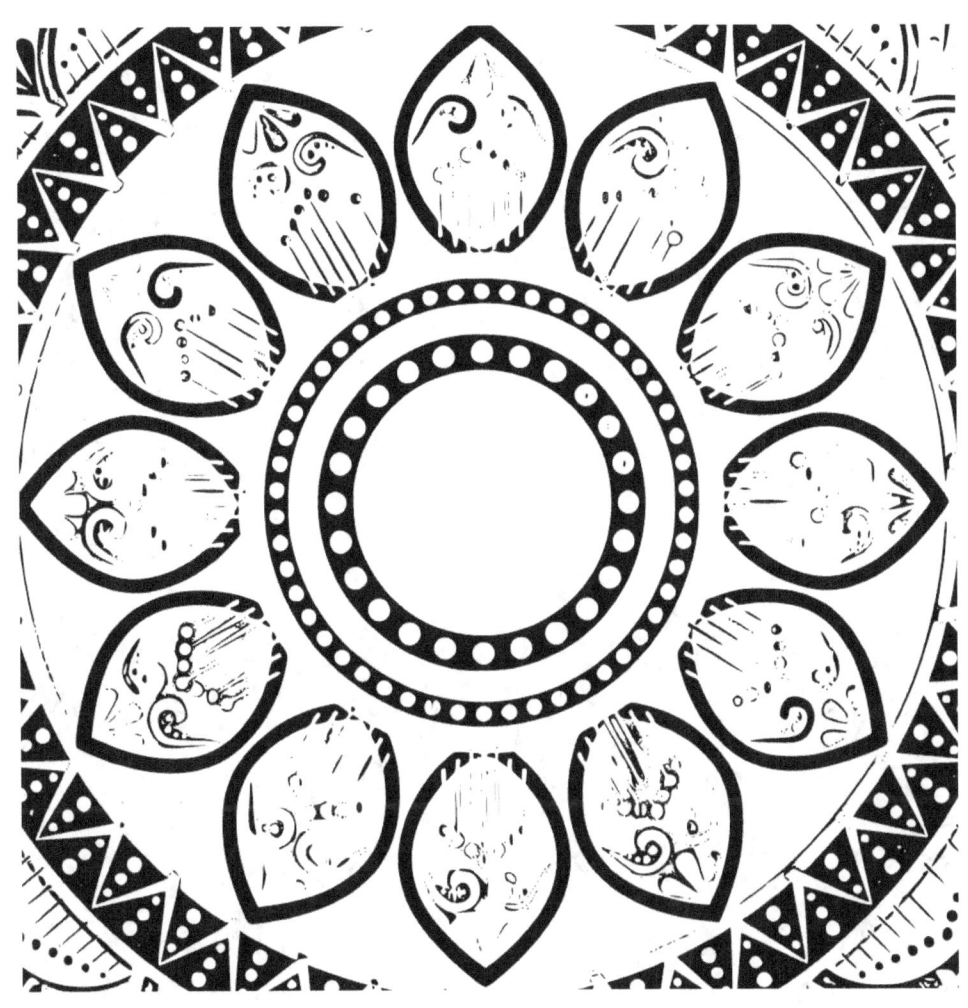

MANDALA
ART

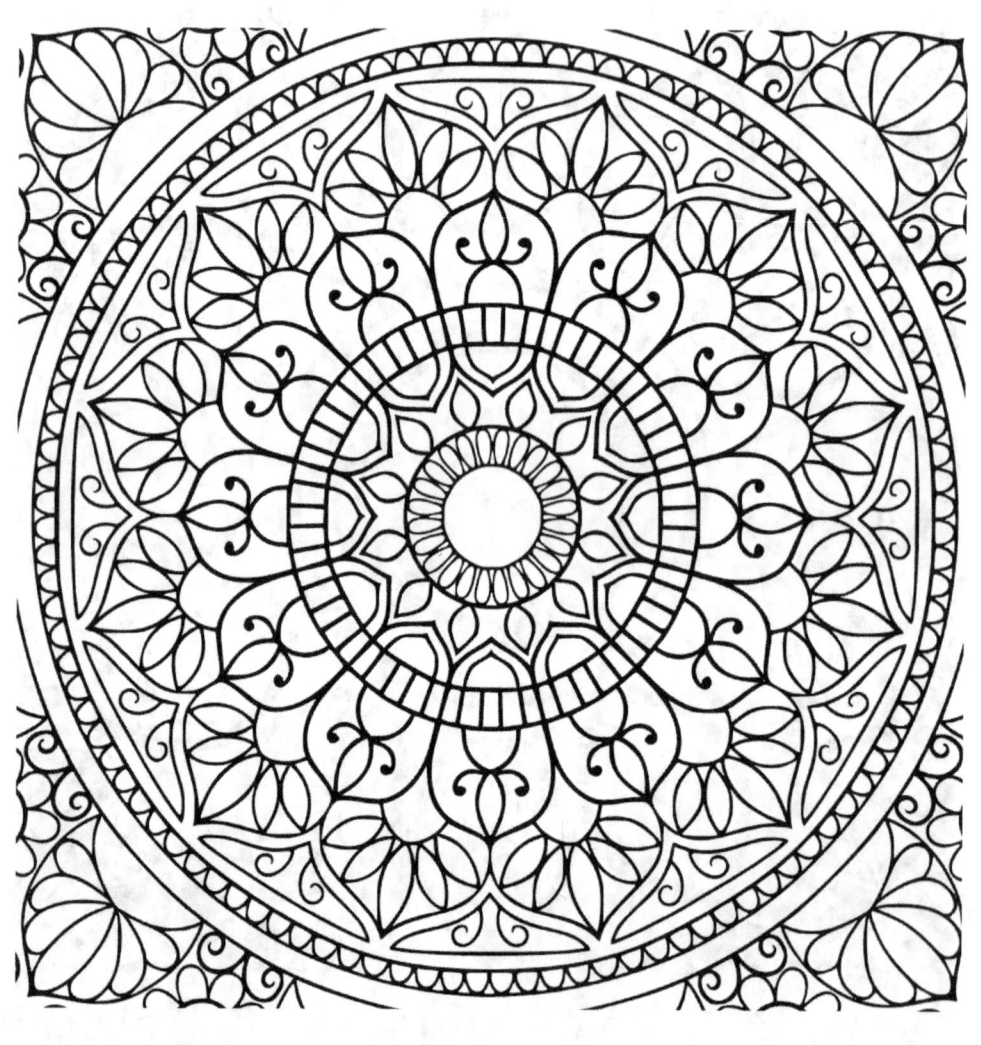

MANDALA

ART

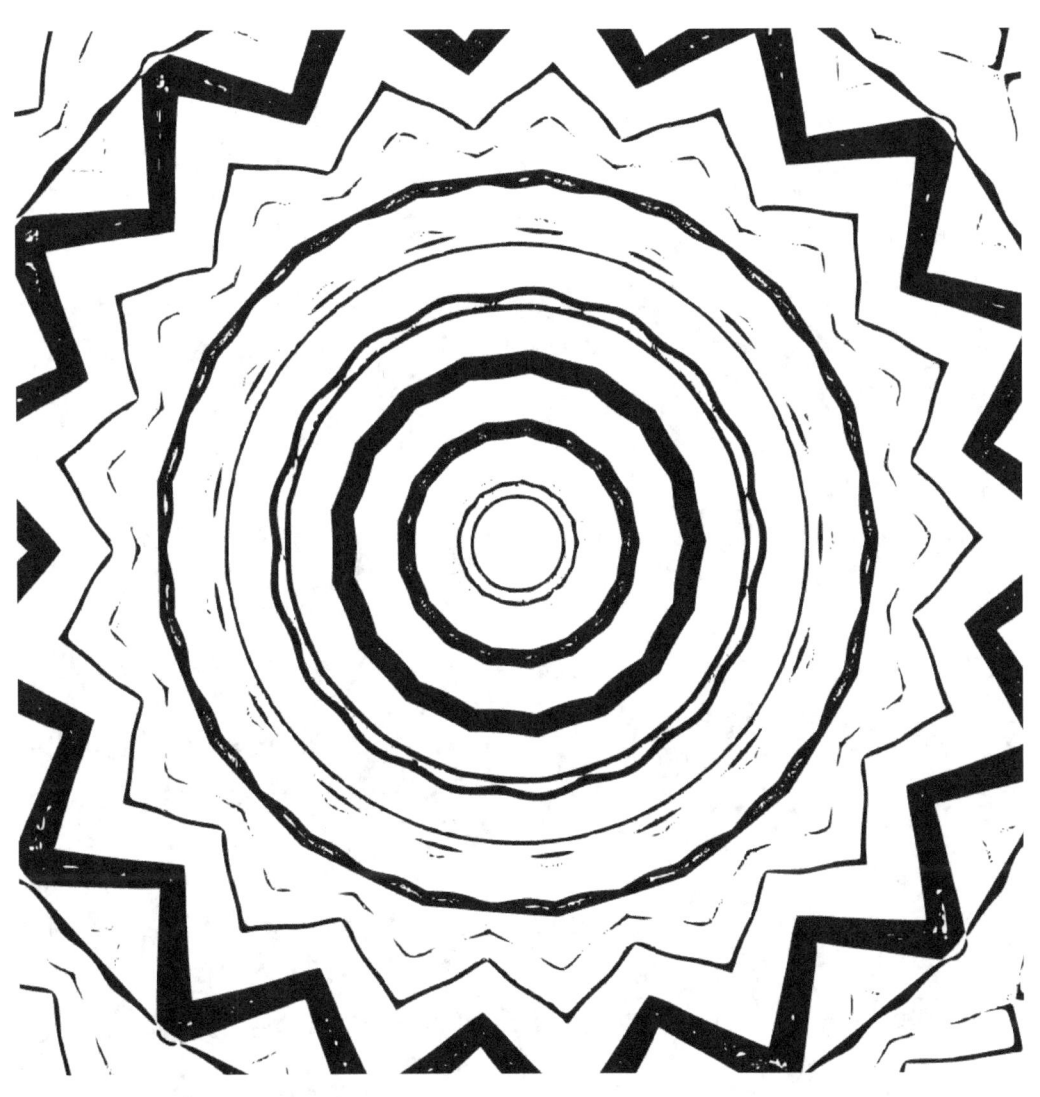

MANDALA ART

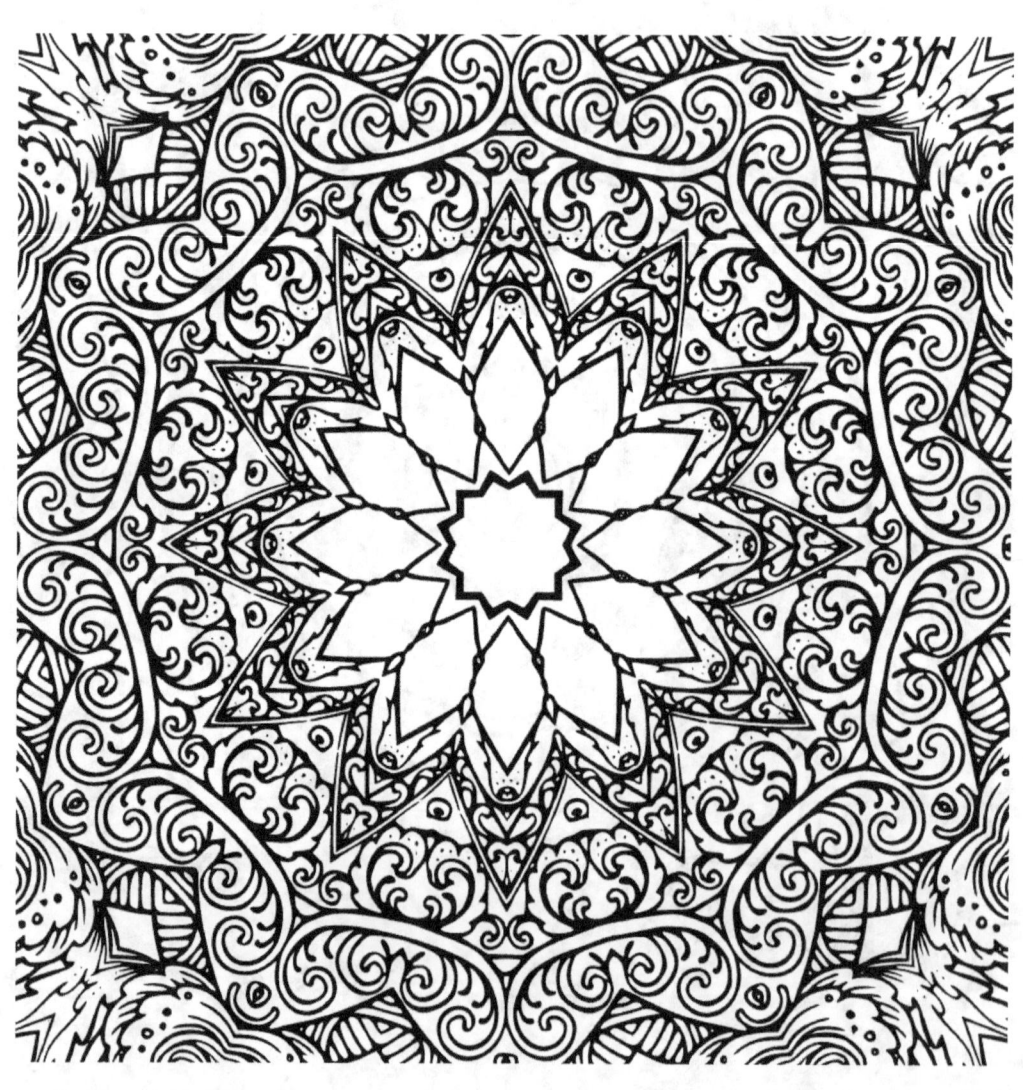

MANDALA
ART

MANDALA
ART

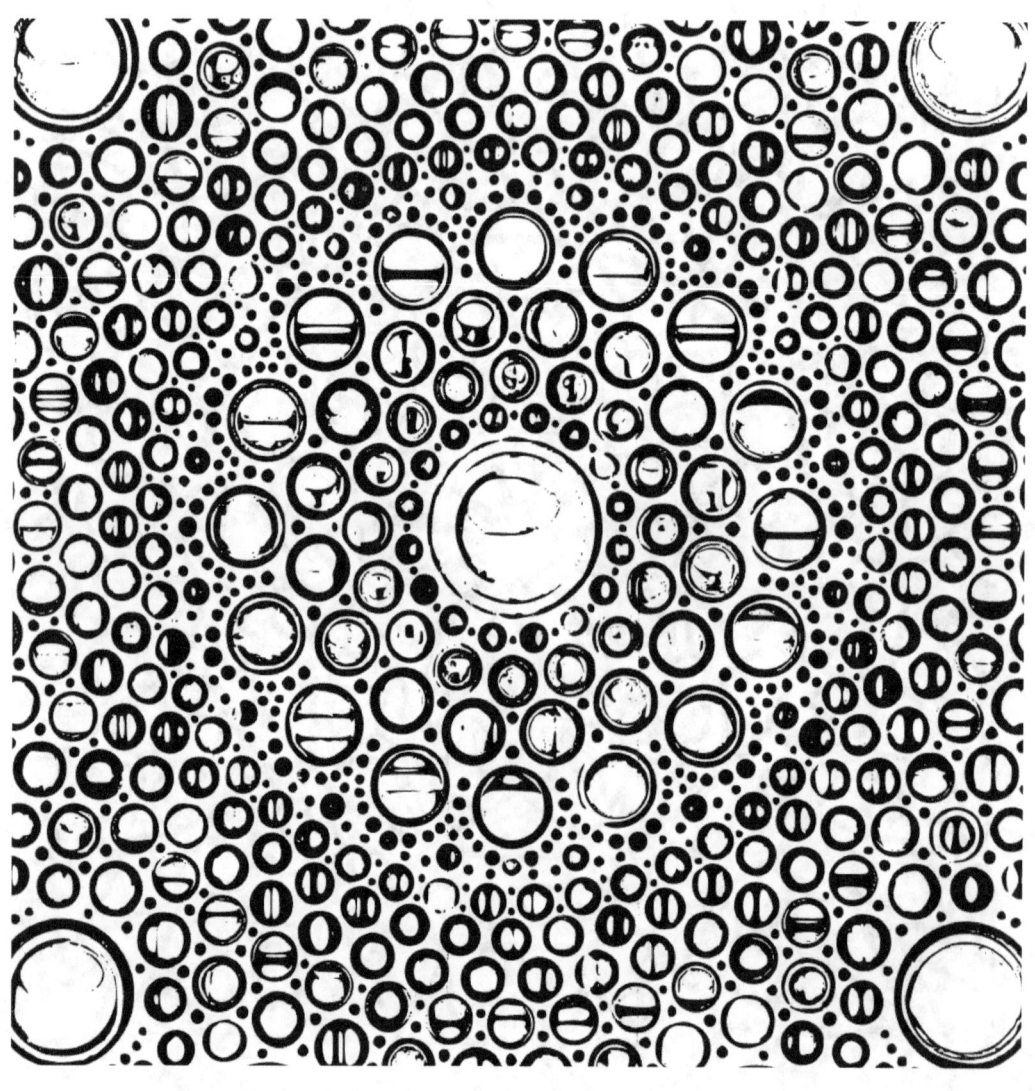

MANDALA

ART

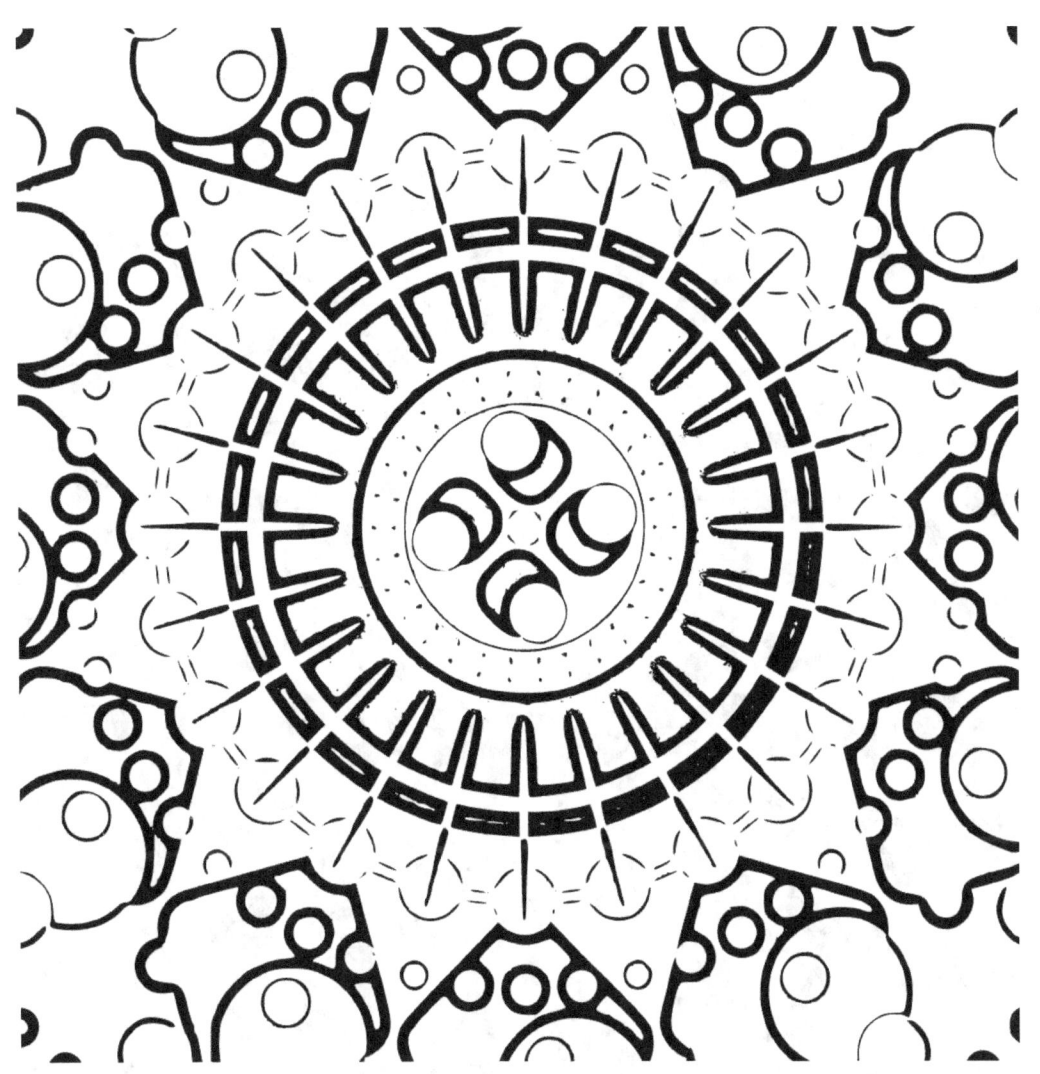

MANDALA
ART

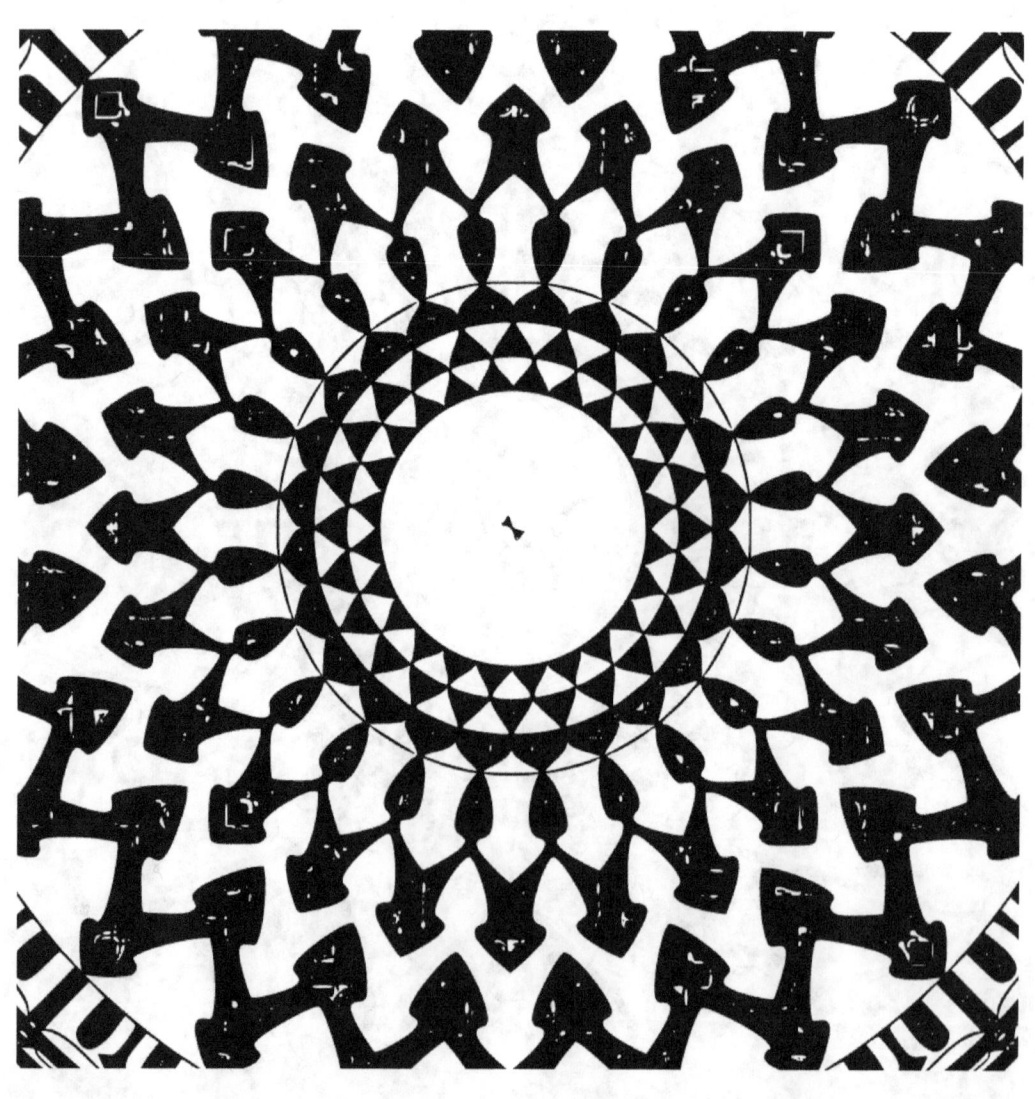

MANDALA
ART

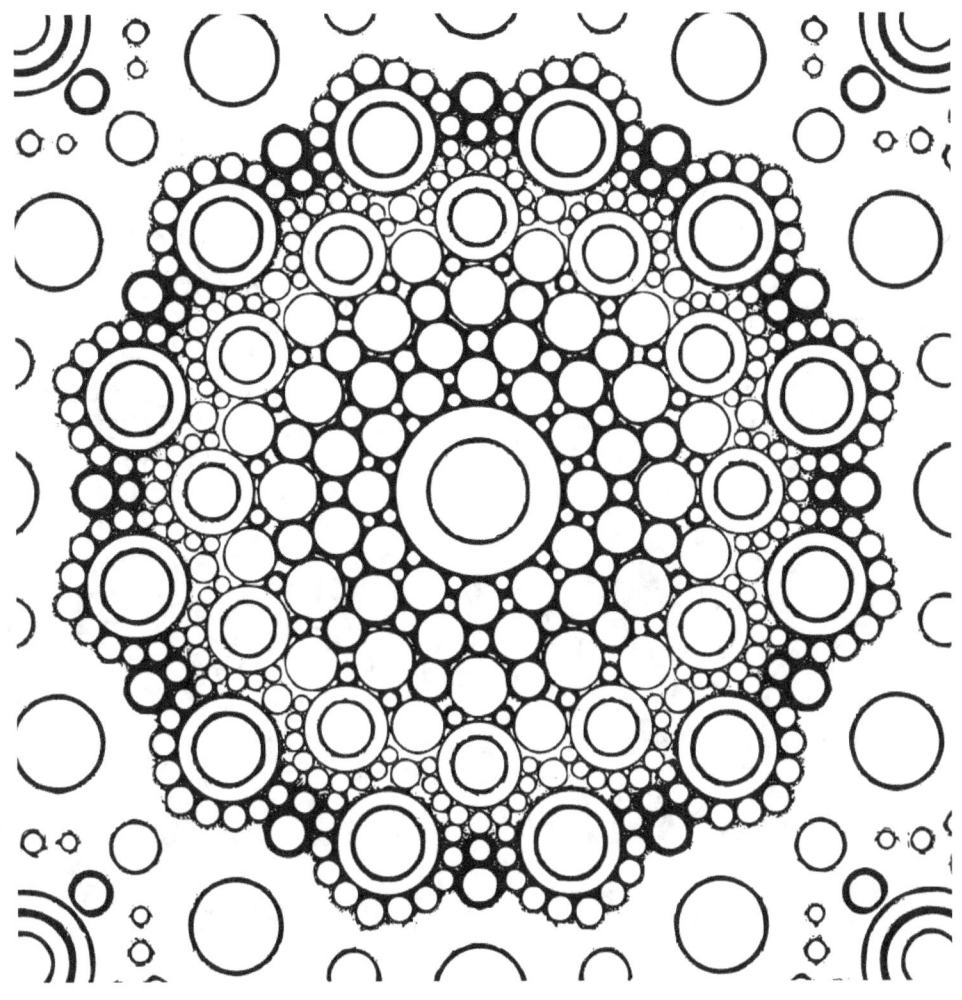

MANDALA
ART

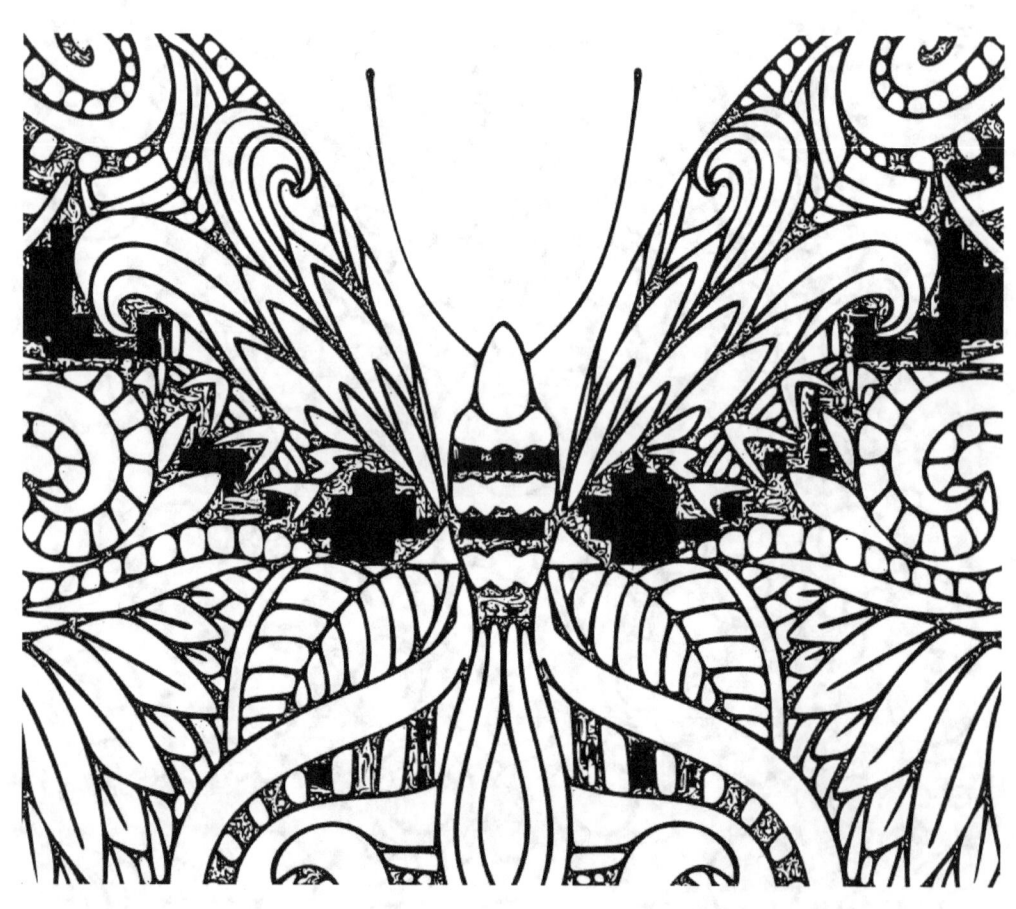

MANDALA
ART

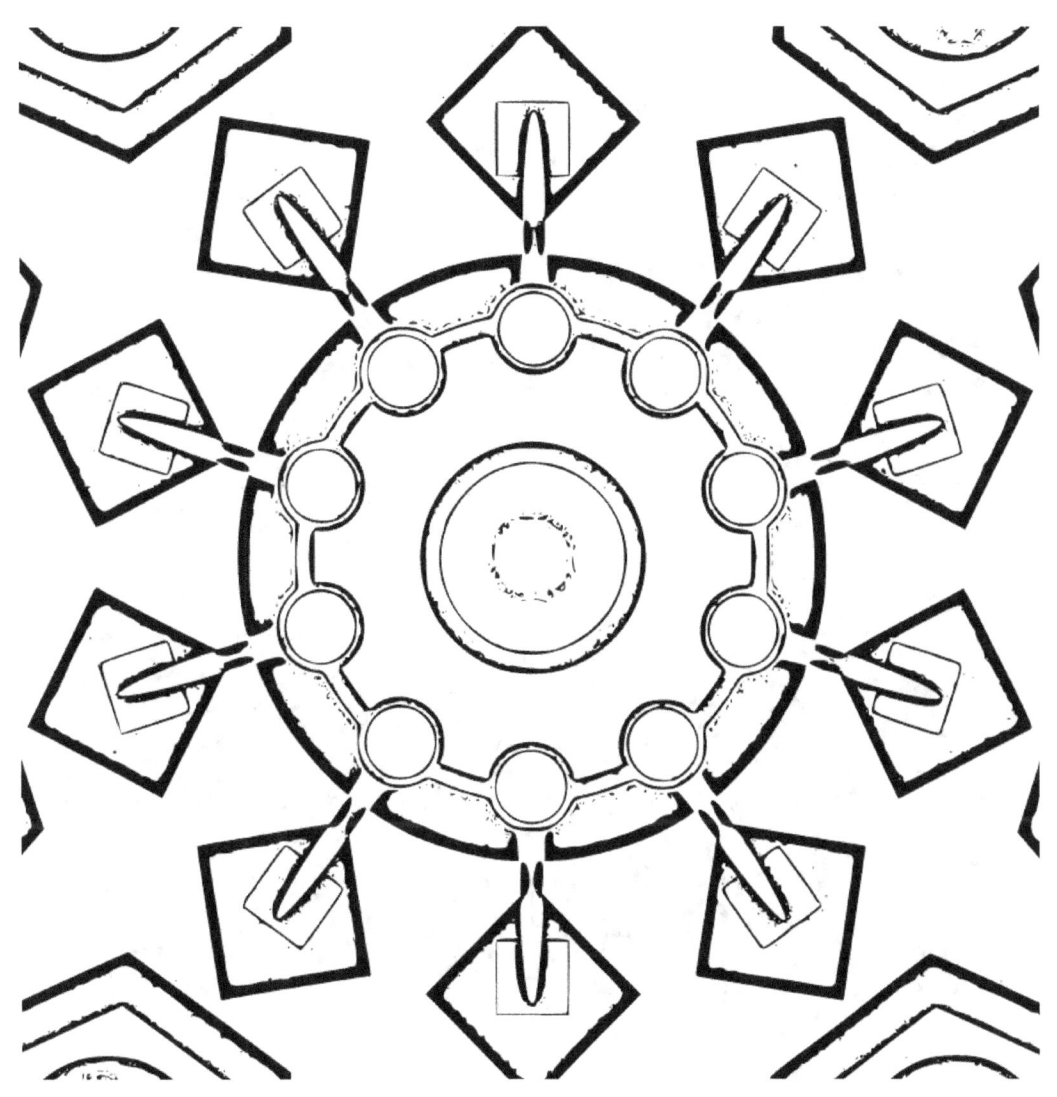

MANDALA
ART

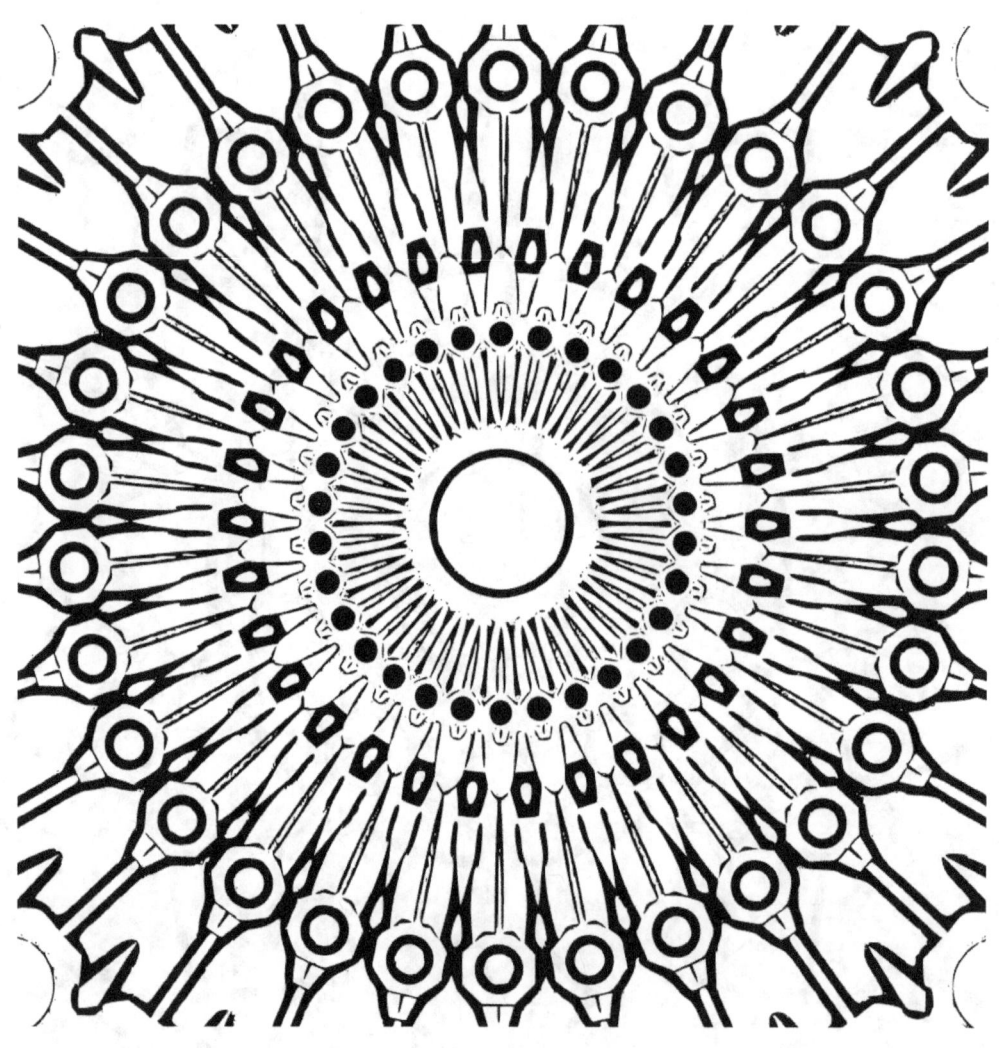

MANDALA
ART

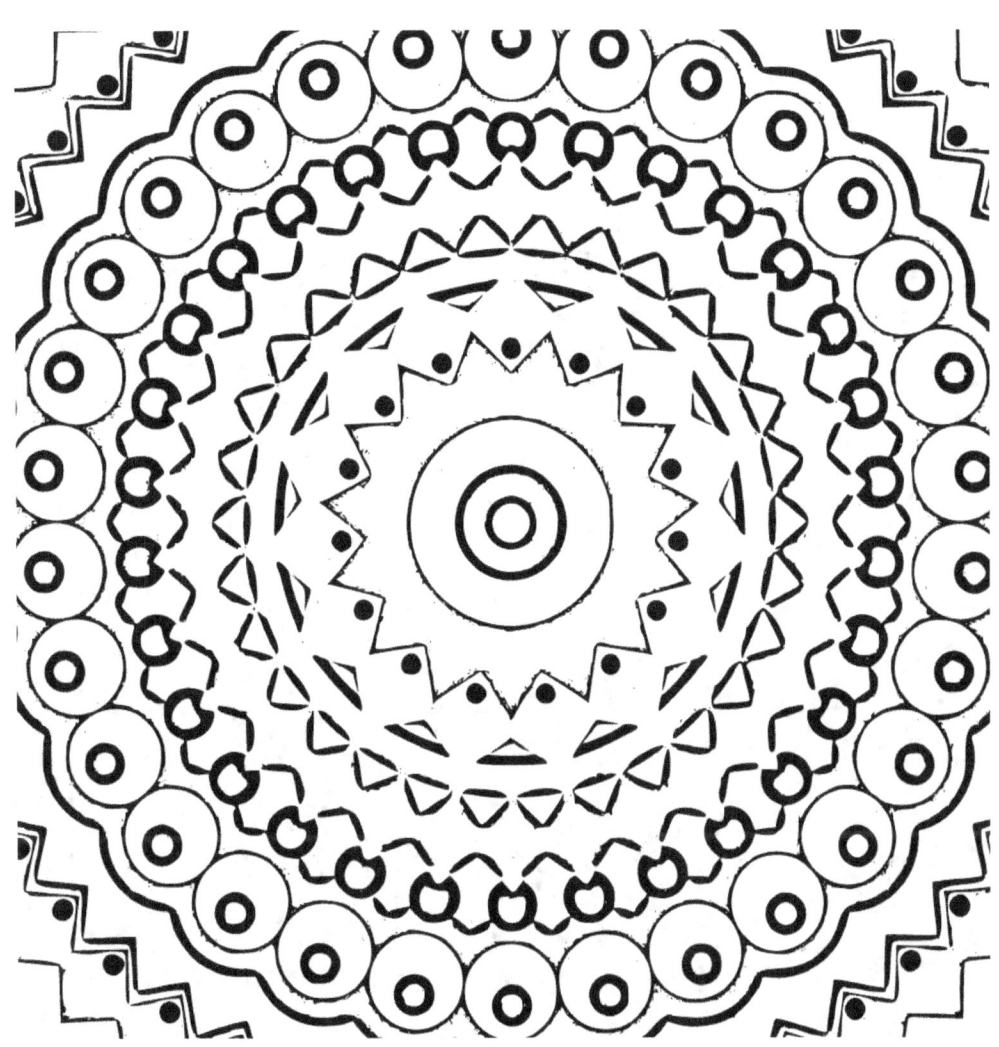

MANDALA

ART

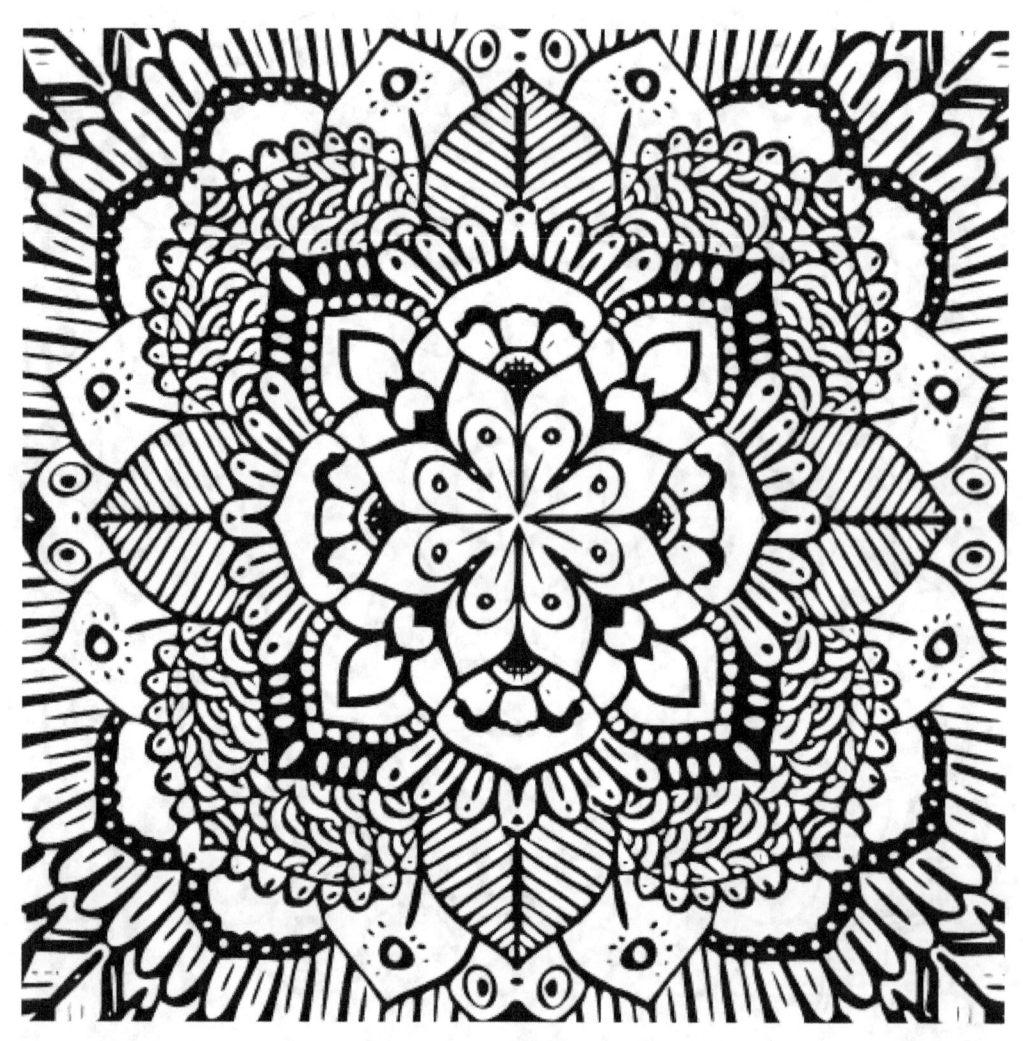

MANDALA
ART

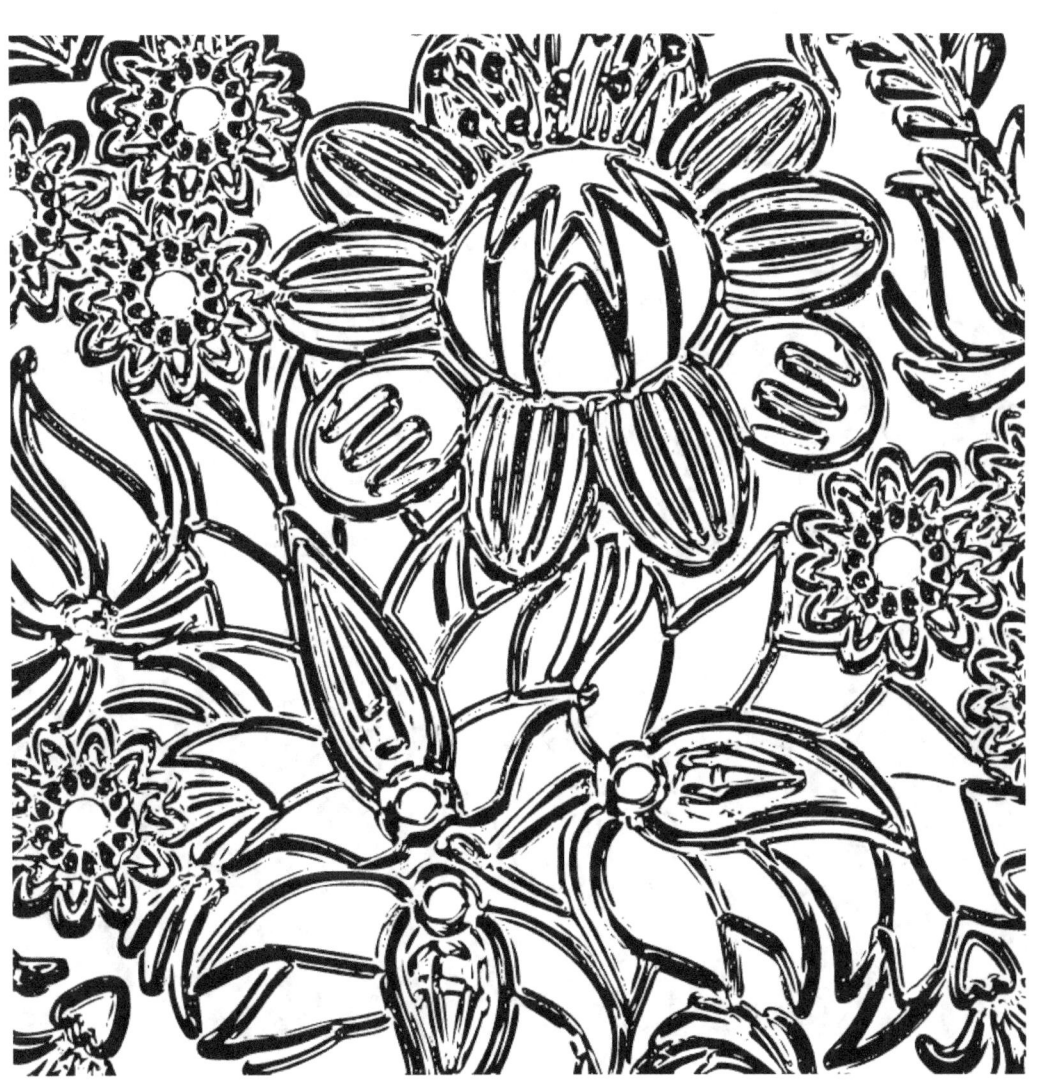

MANDALA
ART

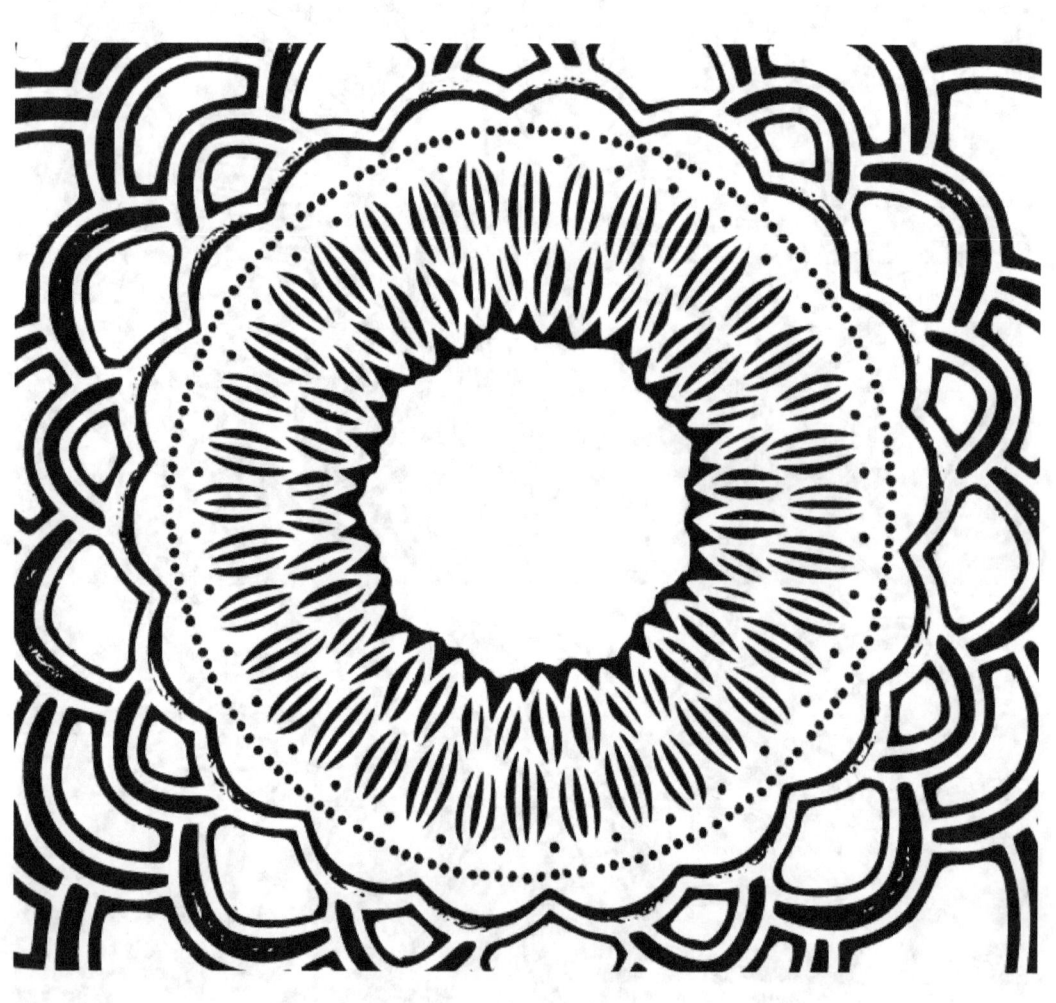

MANDALA ART

MANDALA
ART

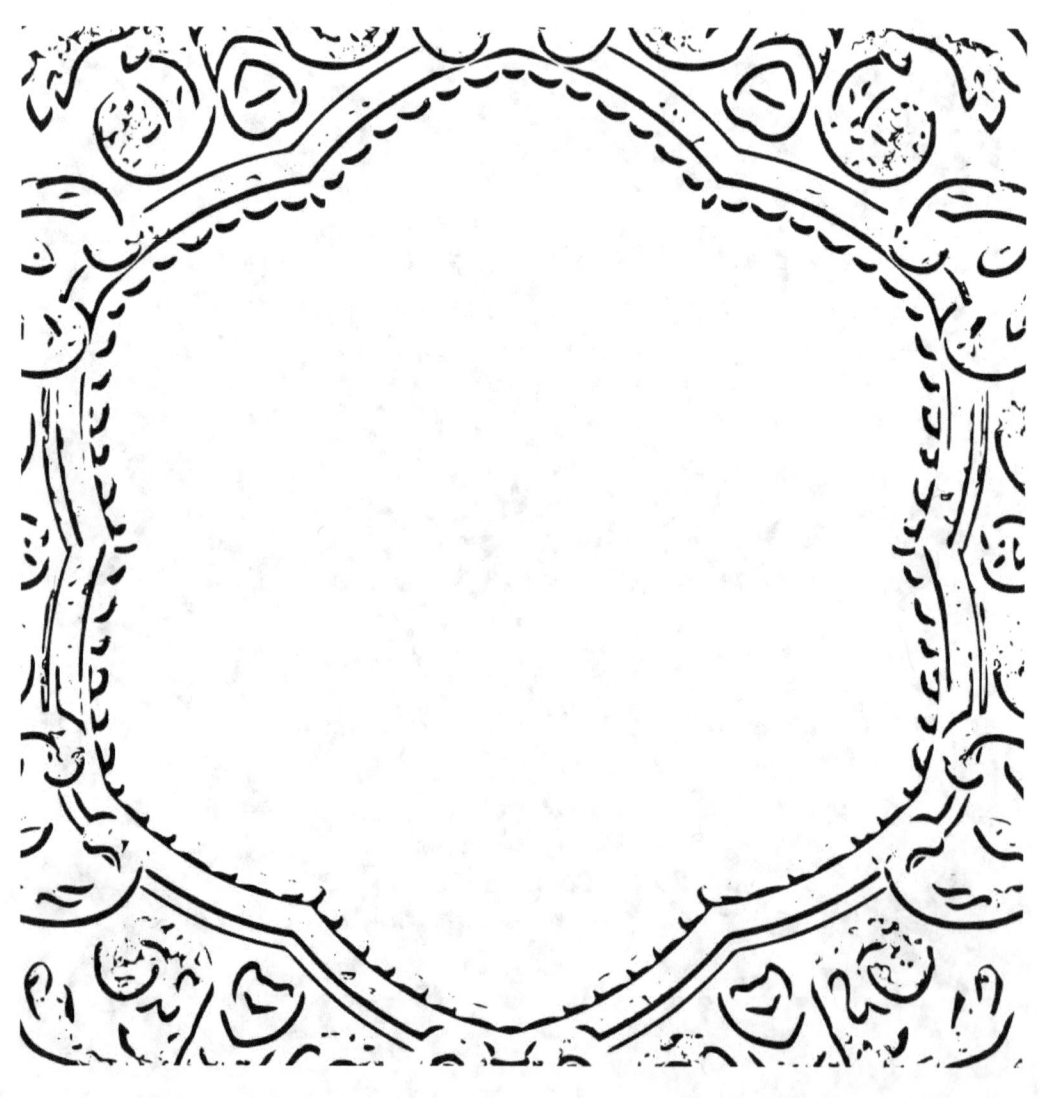

MANDALA

ART

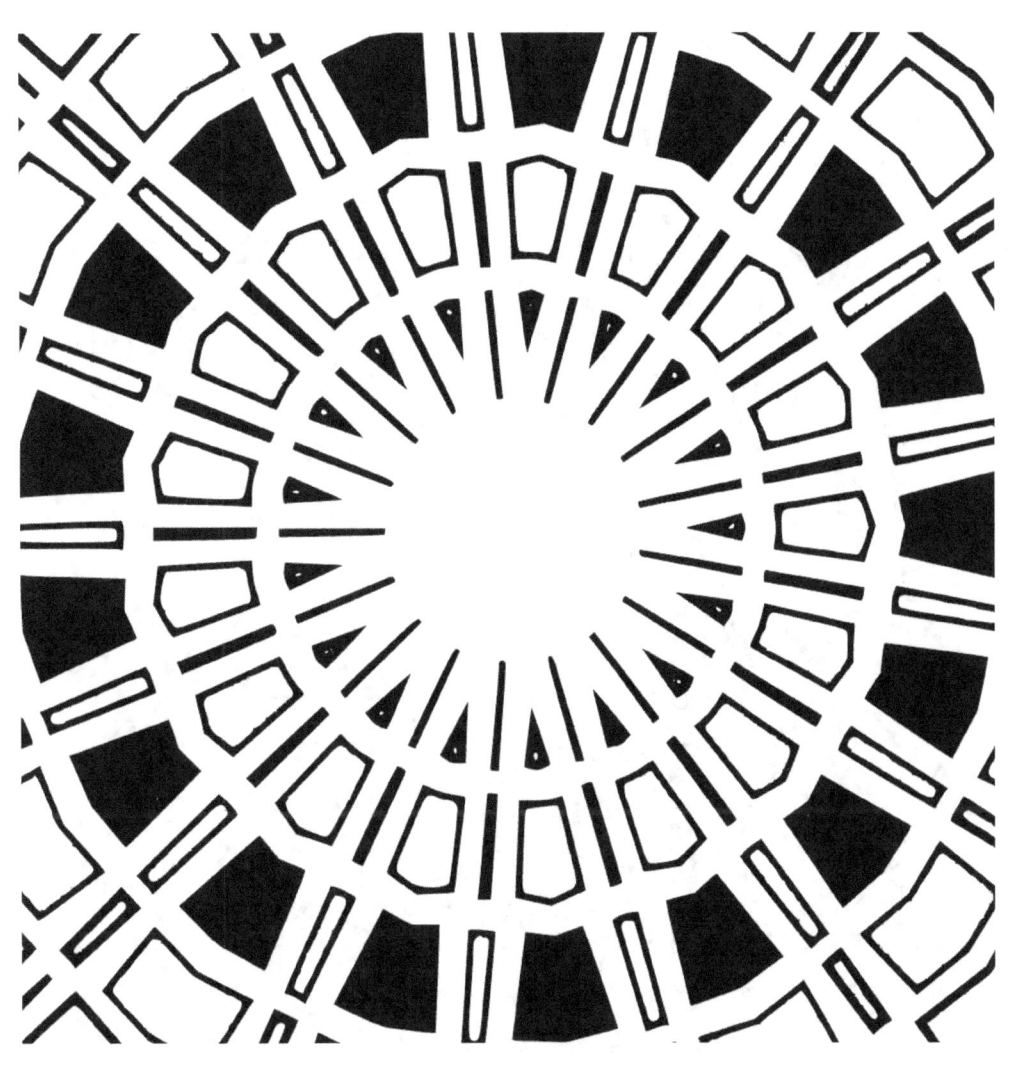

MANDALA ART

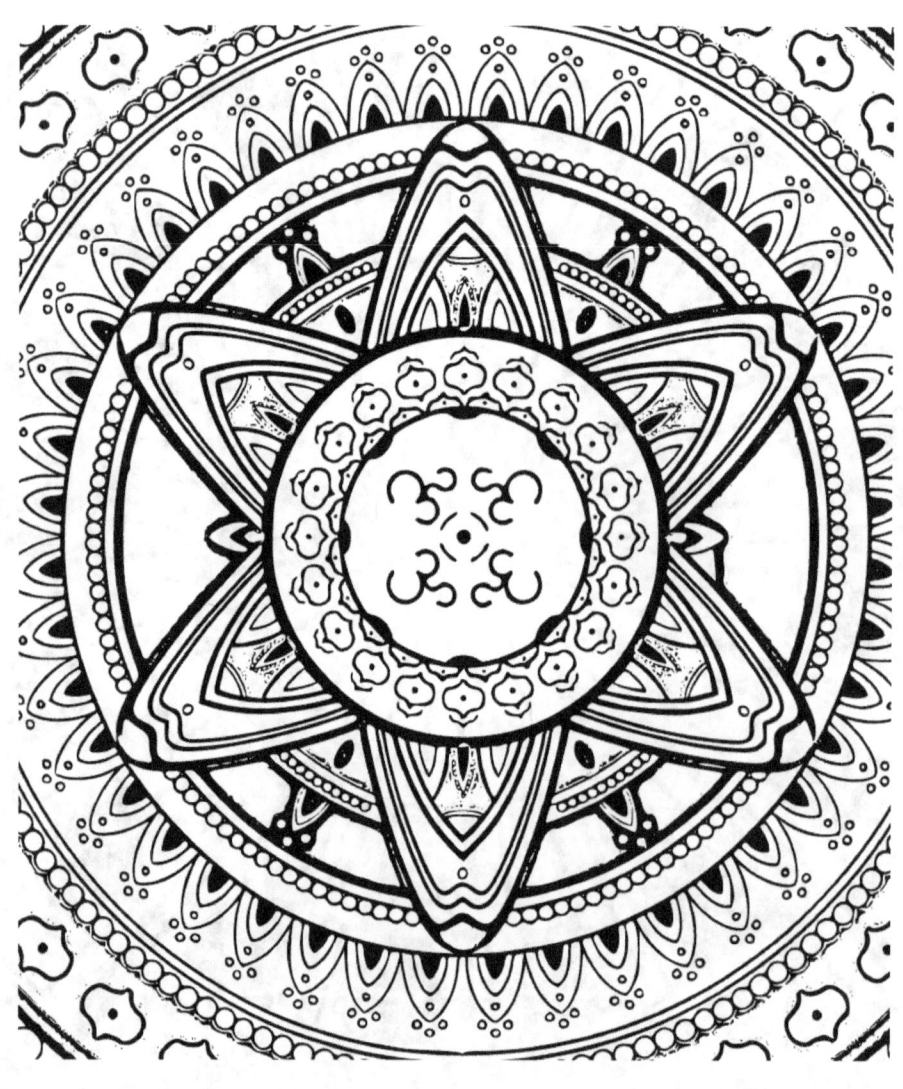

MANDALA
ART

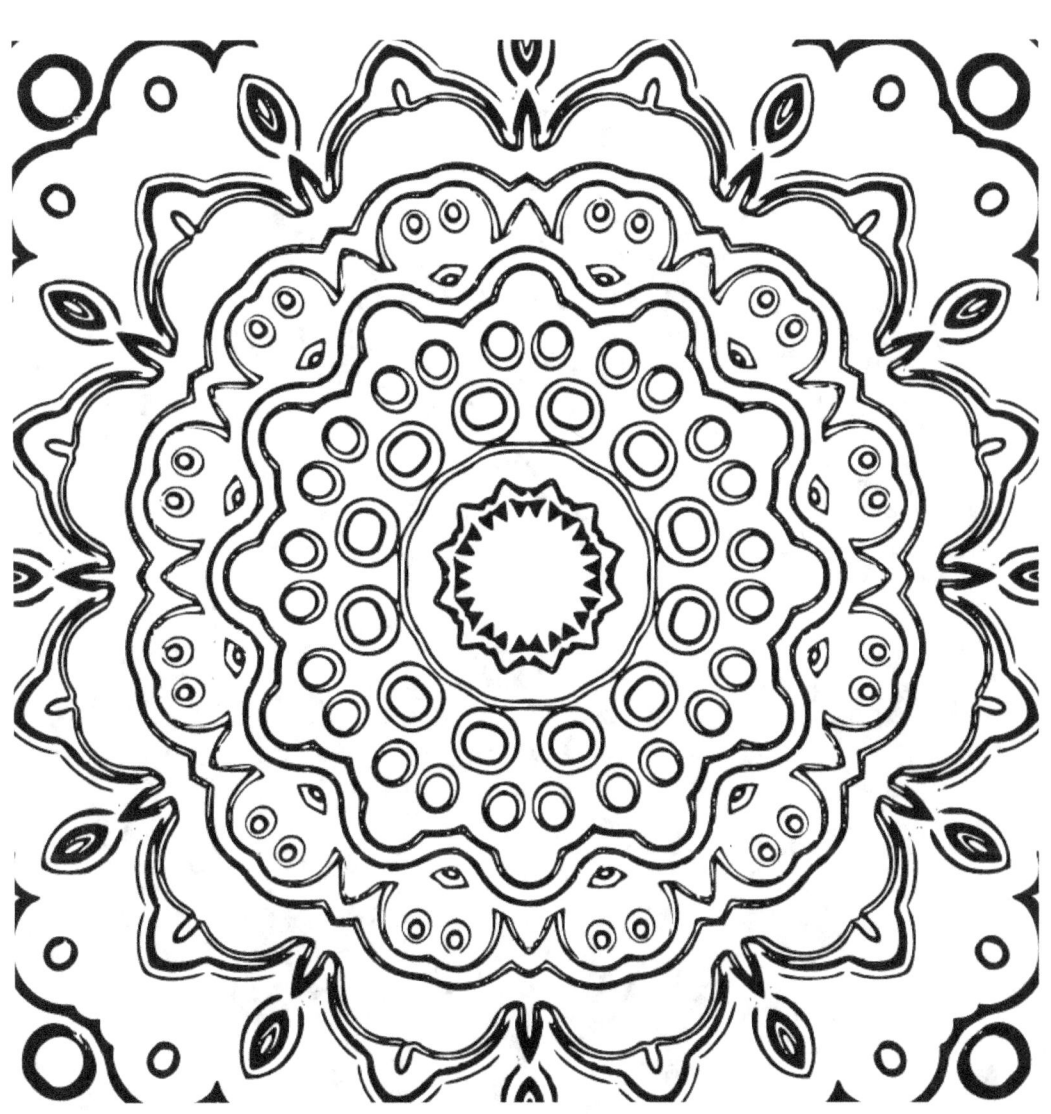

MANDALA
ART

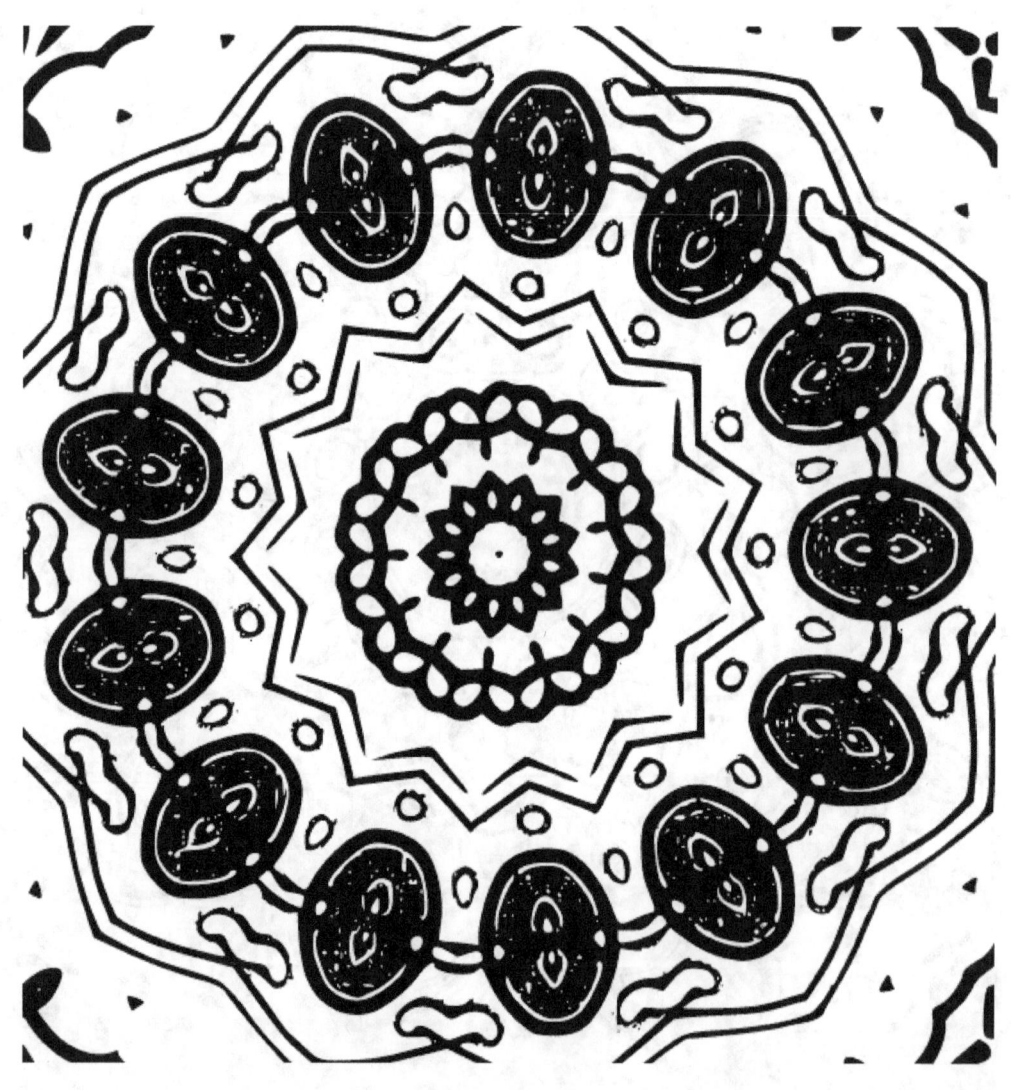

MANDALA
ART

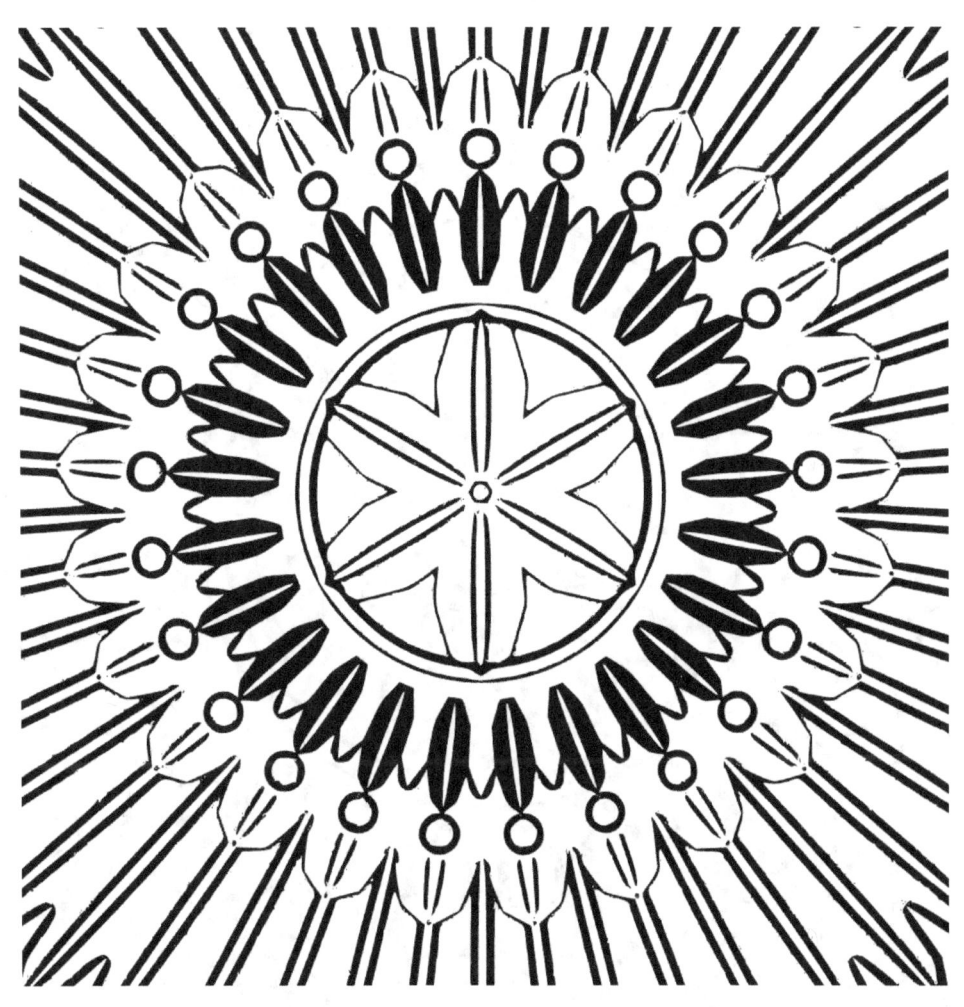

MANDALA
ART

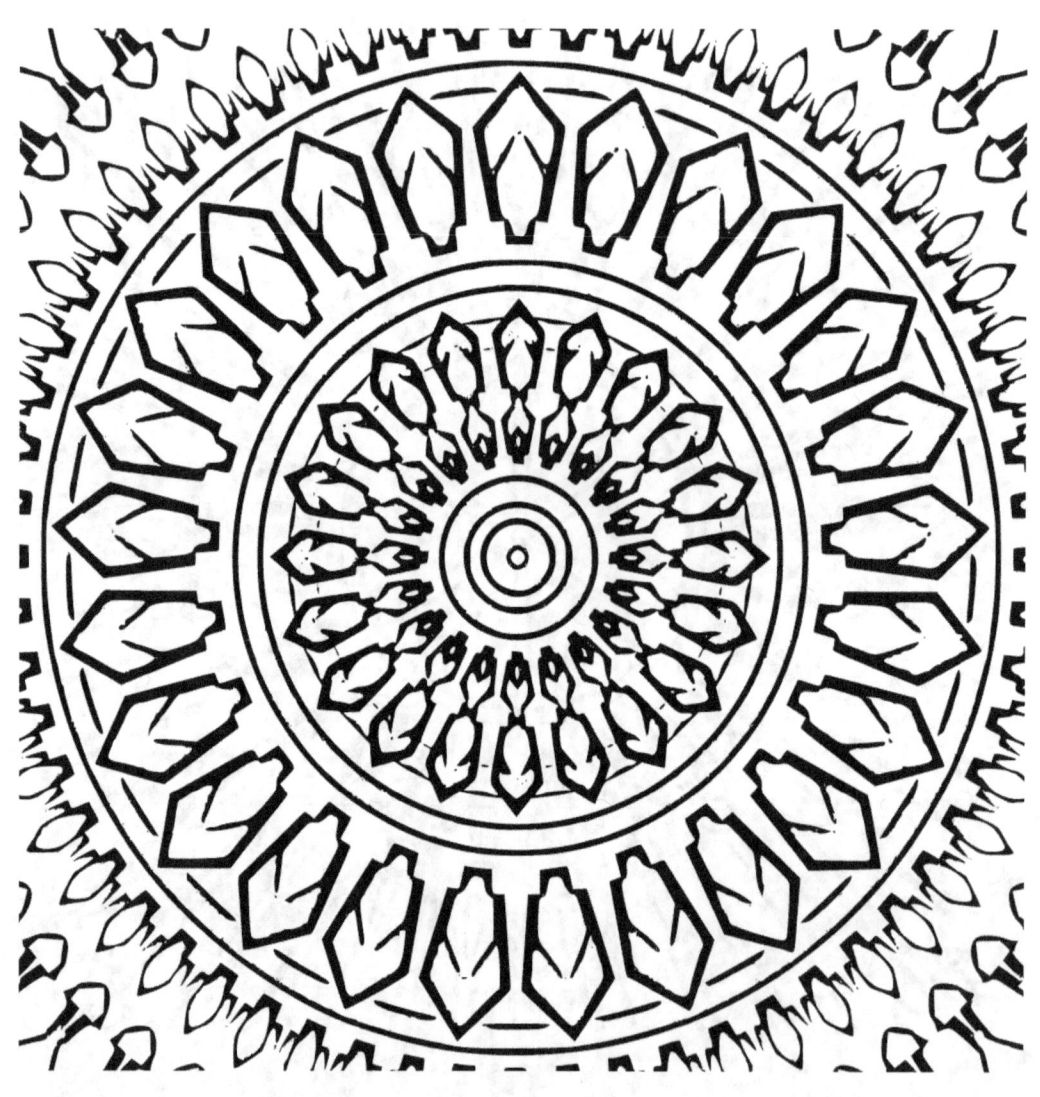

MANDALA

ART

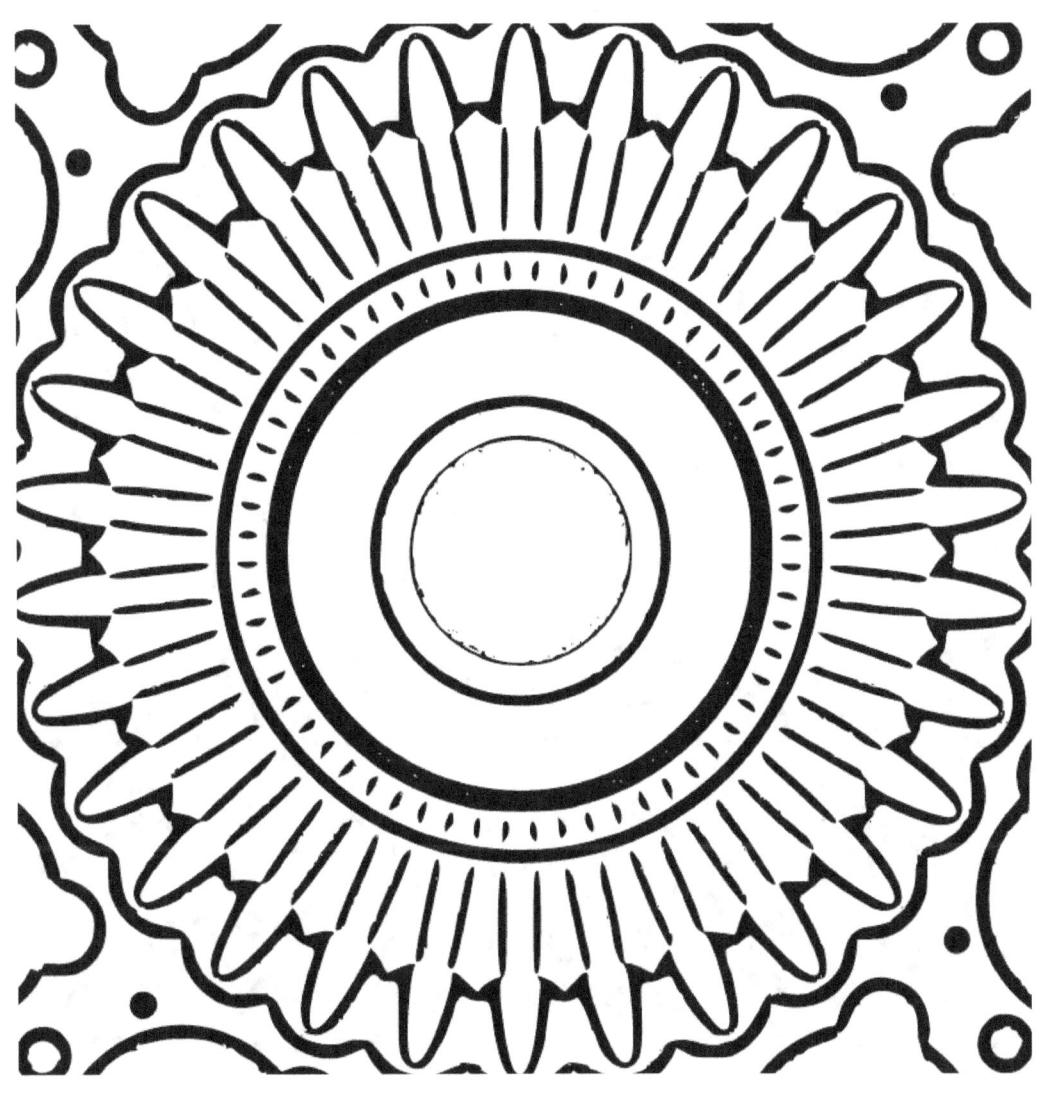

MANDALA

ART

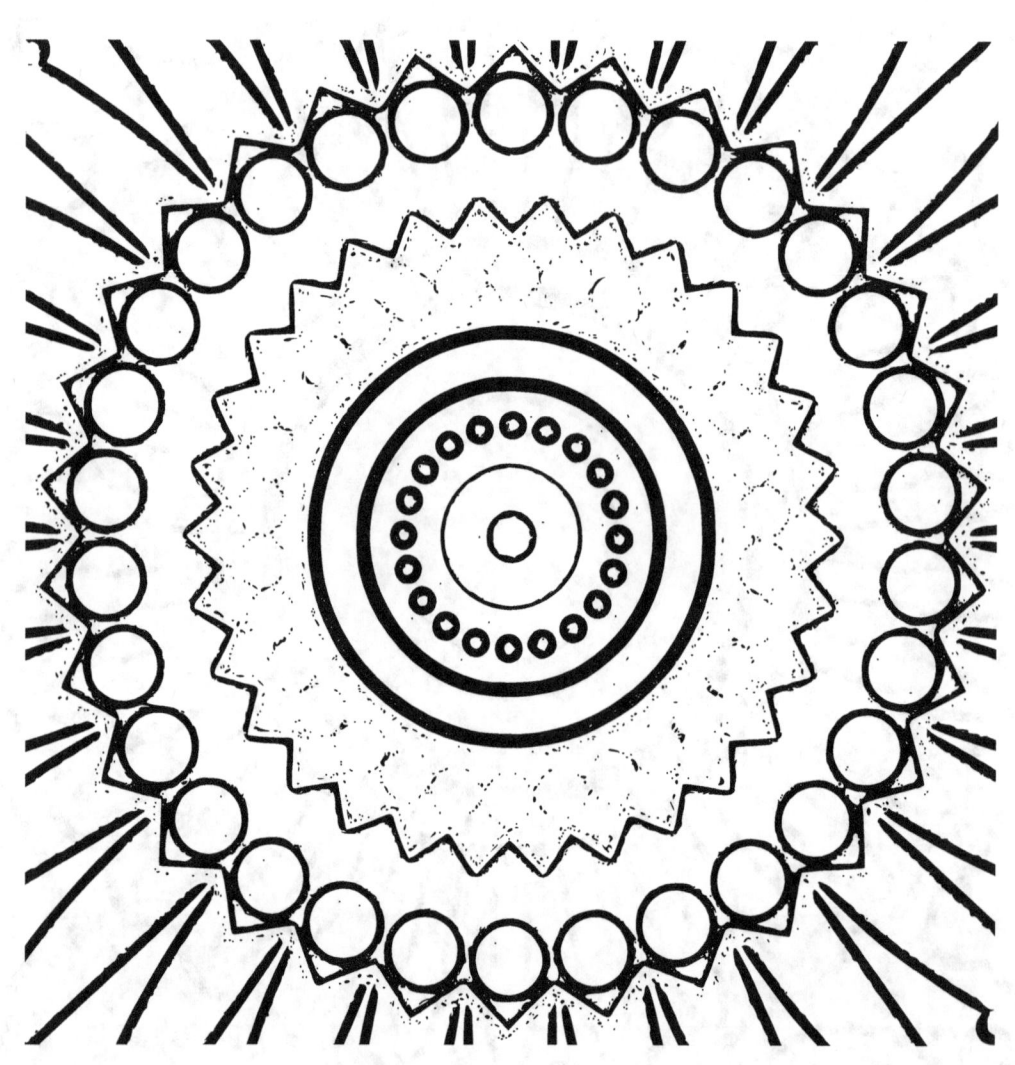

MANDALA
ART

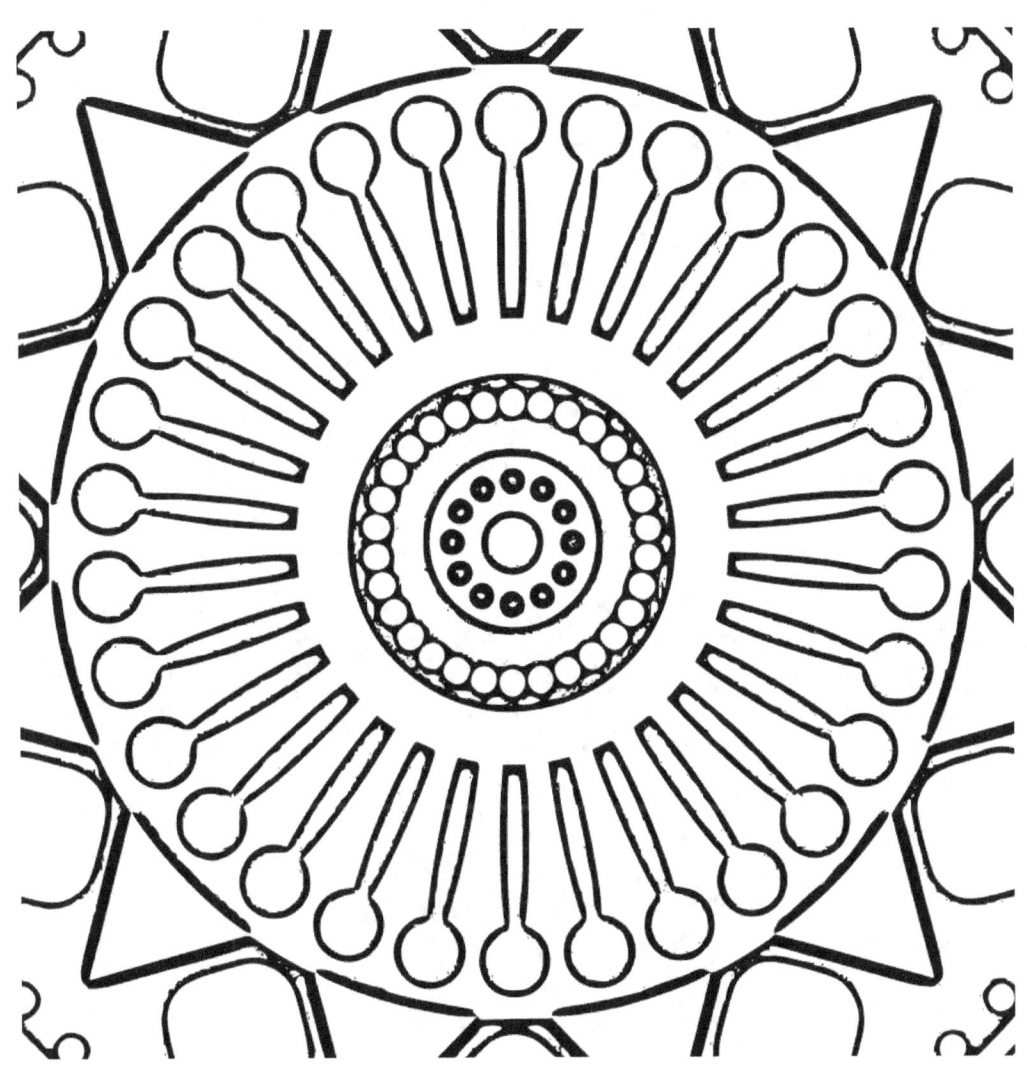

MANDALA
ART

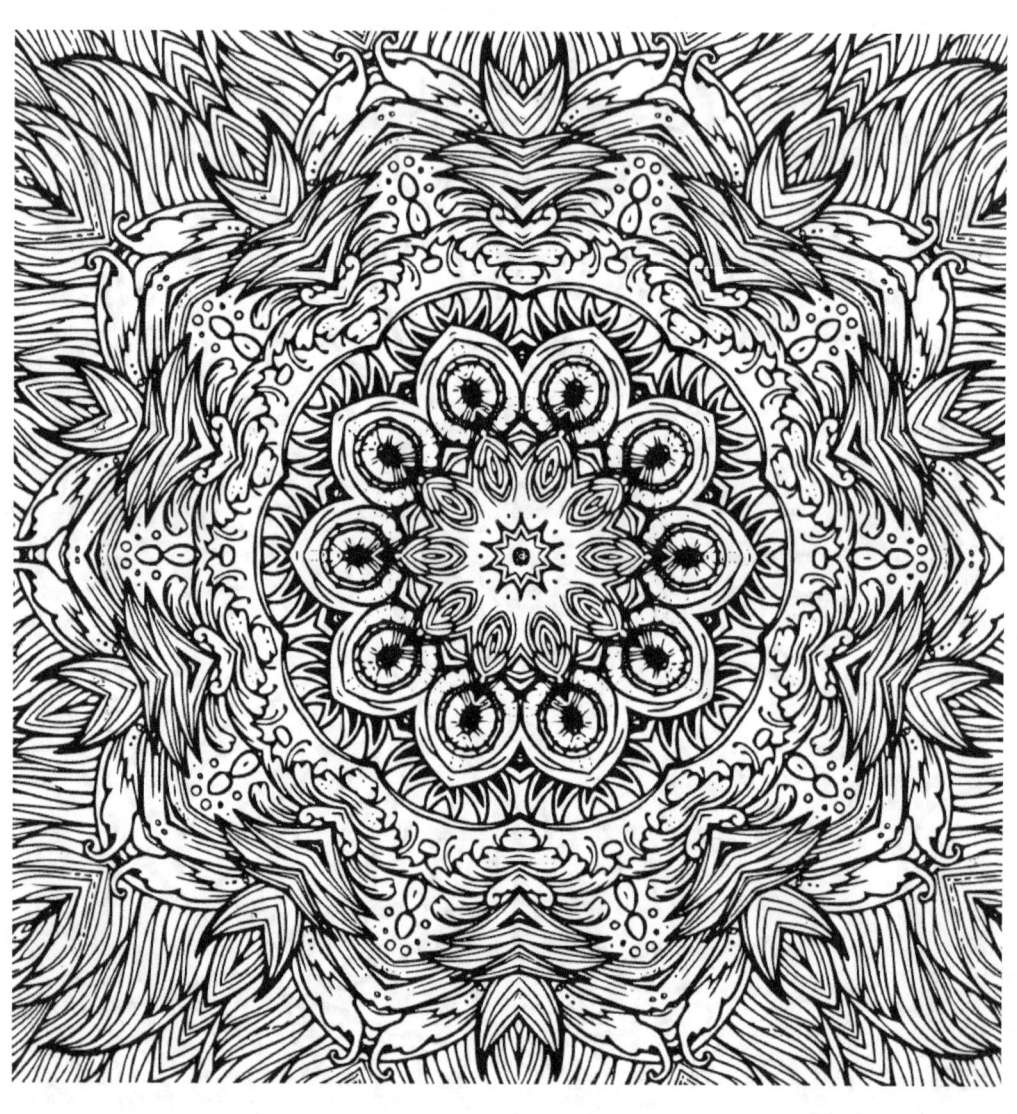

MANDALA

ART

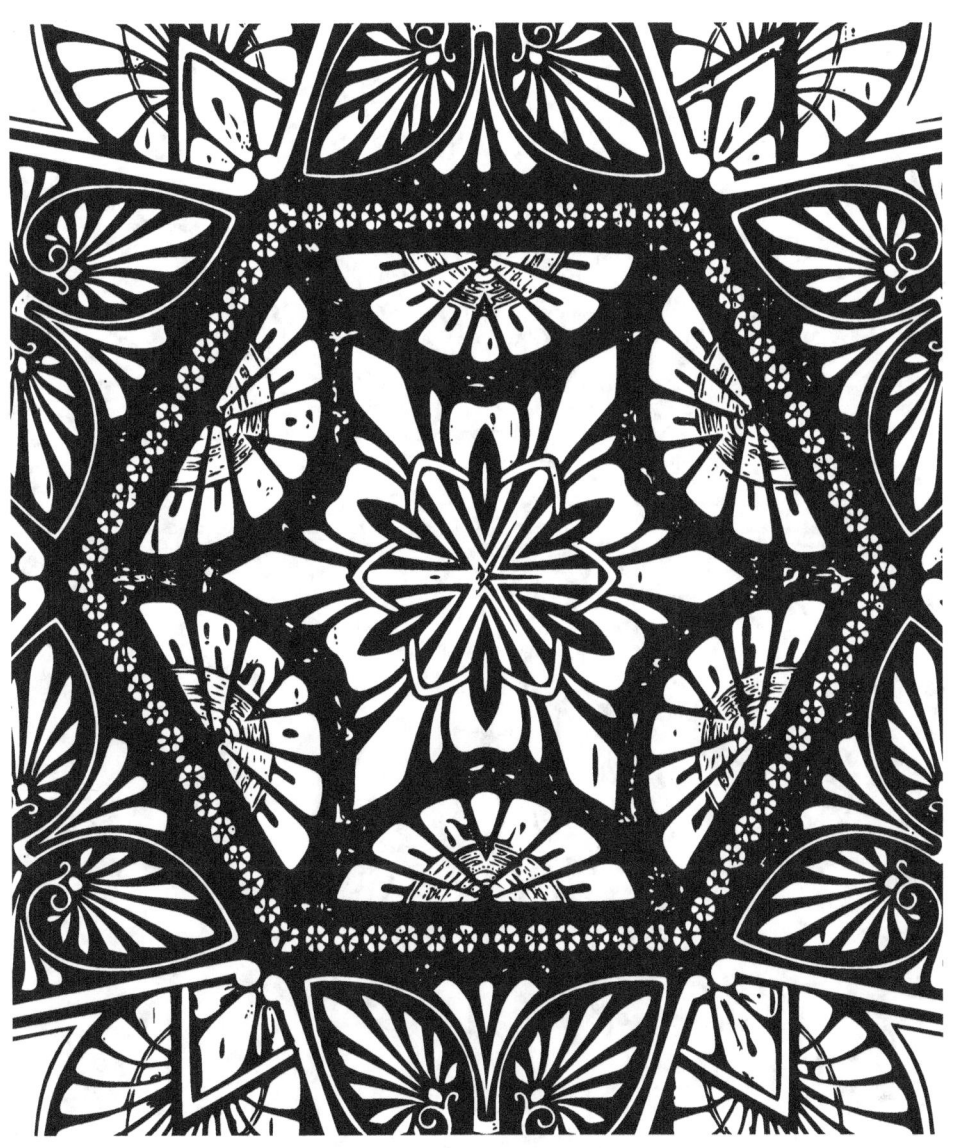

MANDALA
ART

MANDALA
ART

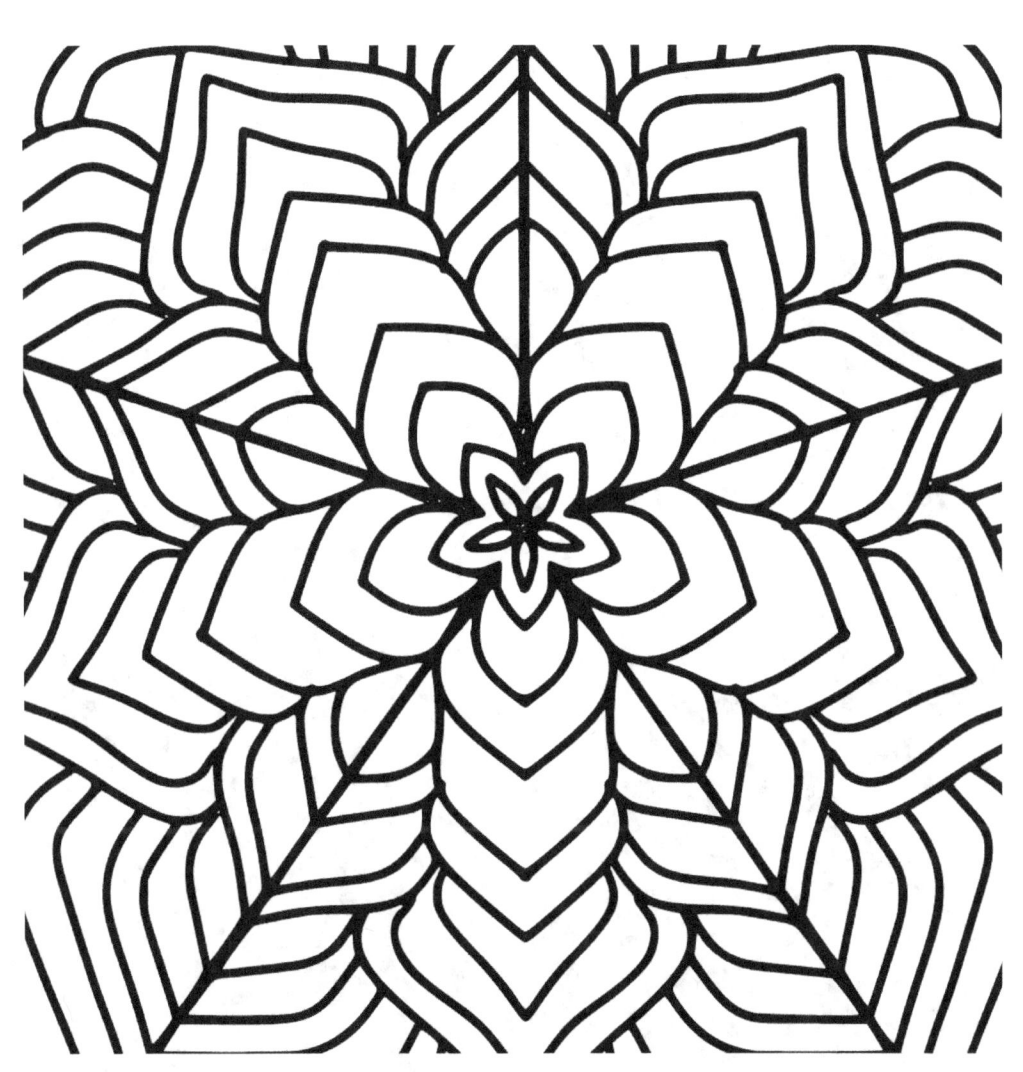

MANDALA
ART

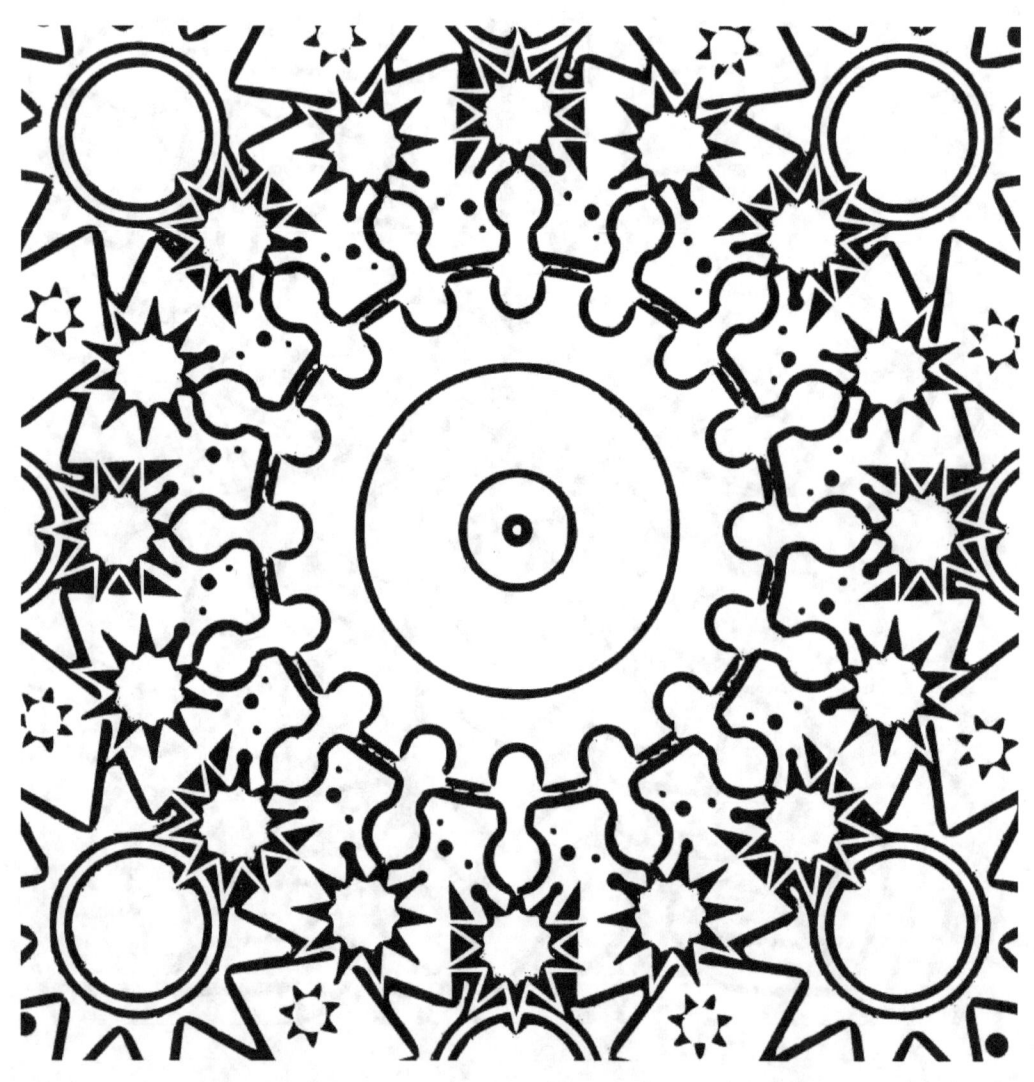

MANDALA
ART

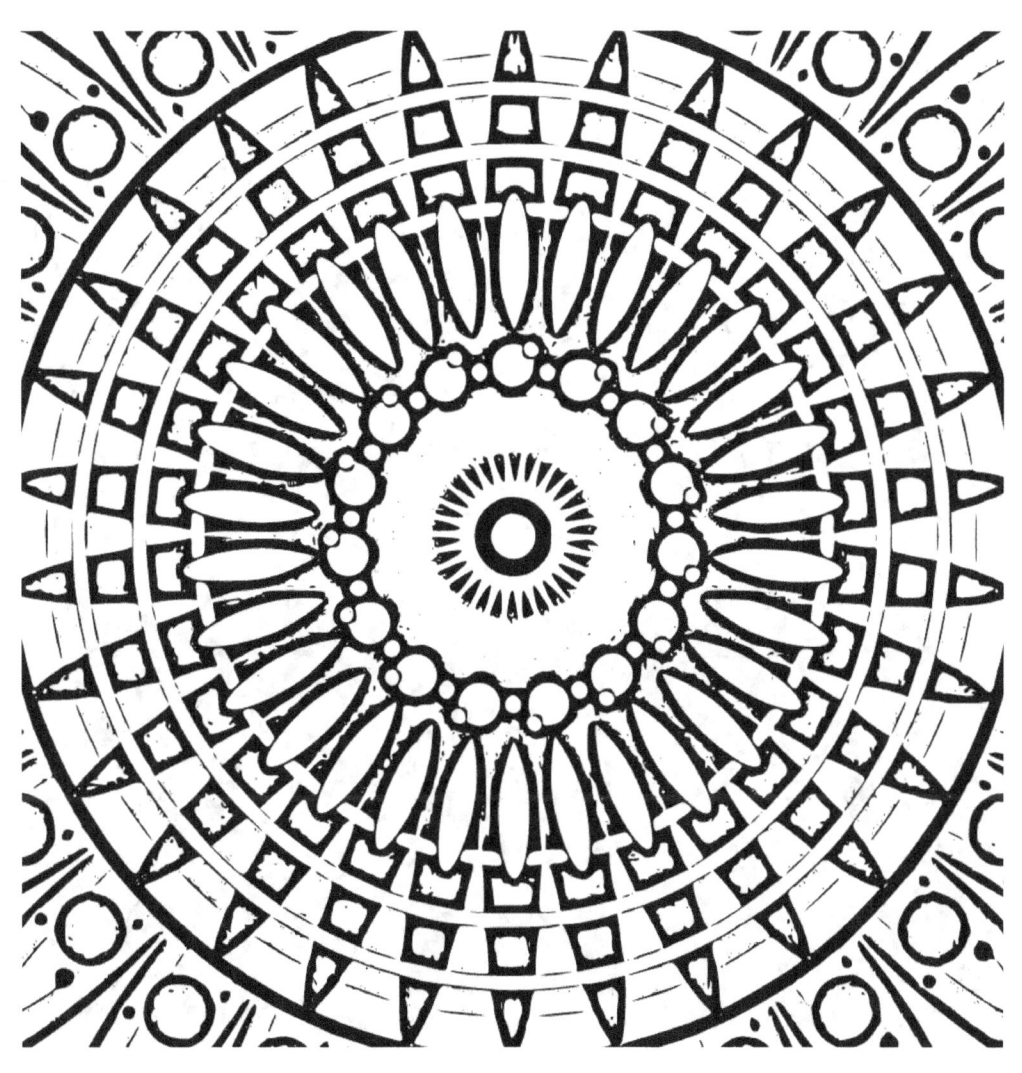

MANDALA
ART

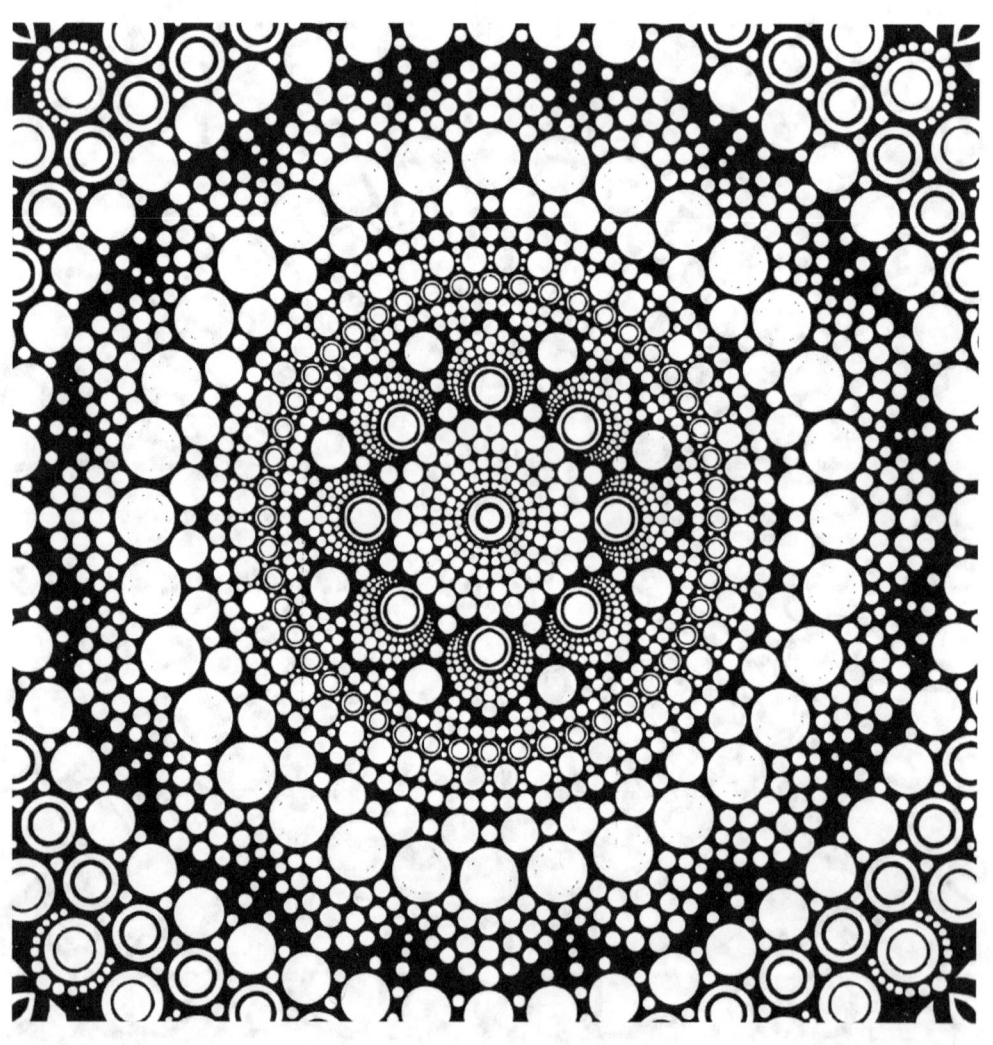

MANDALA

ART

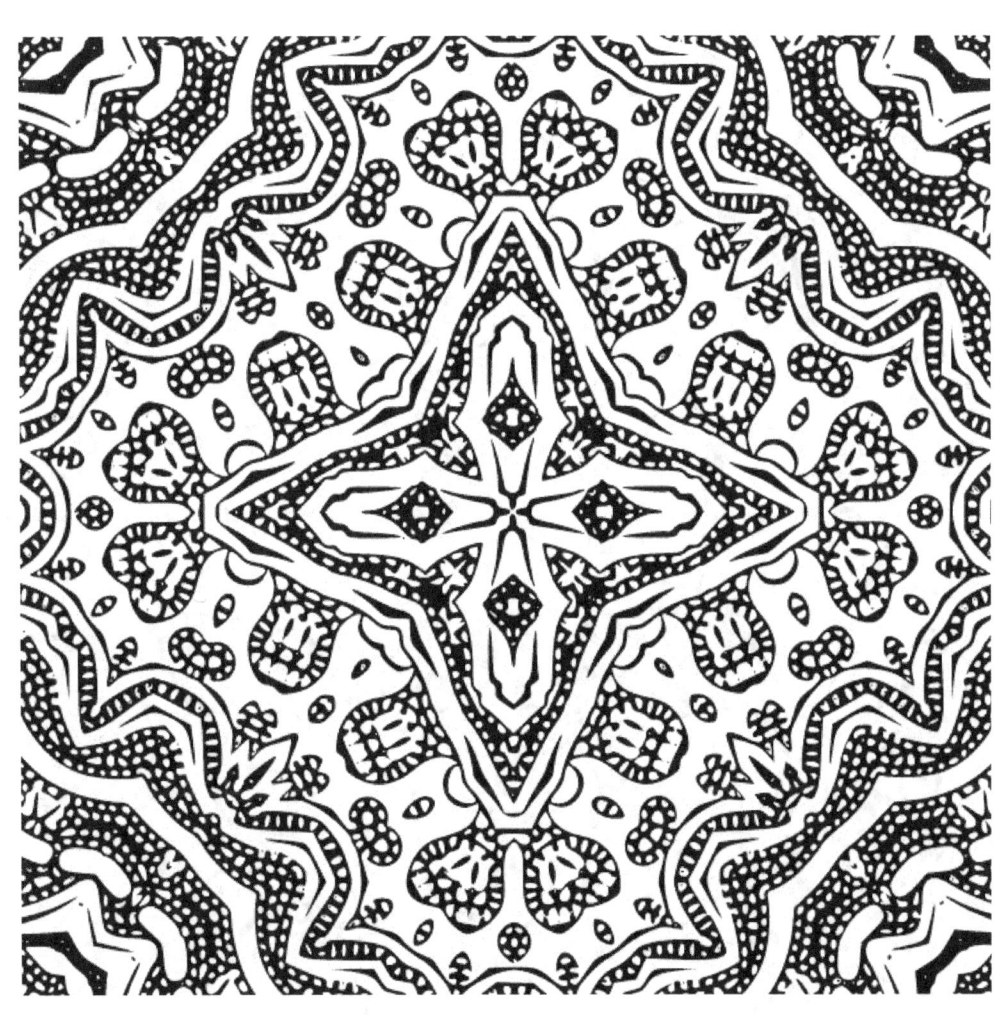

MANDALA
ART

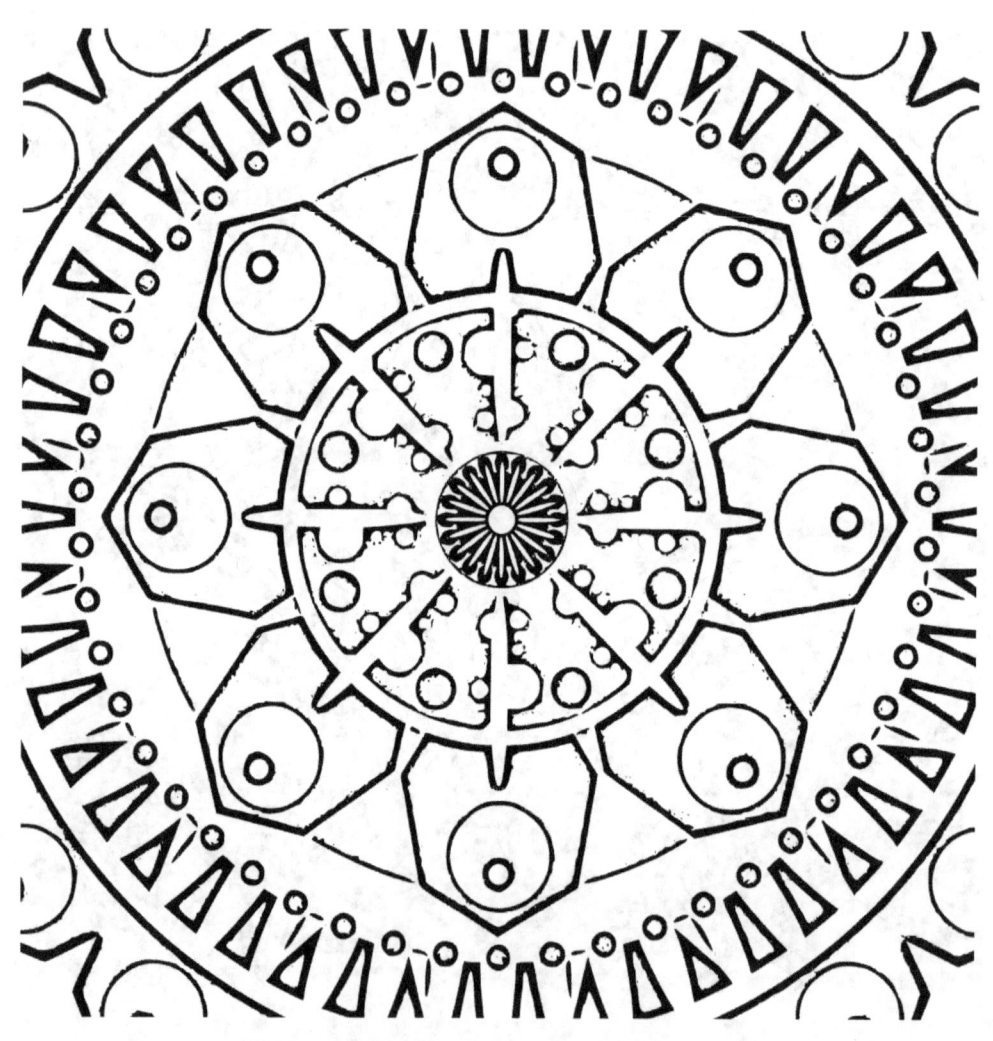

MANDALA
ART

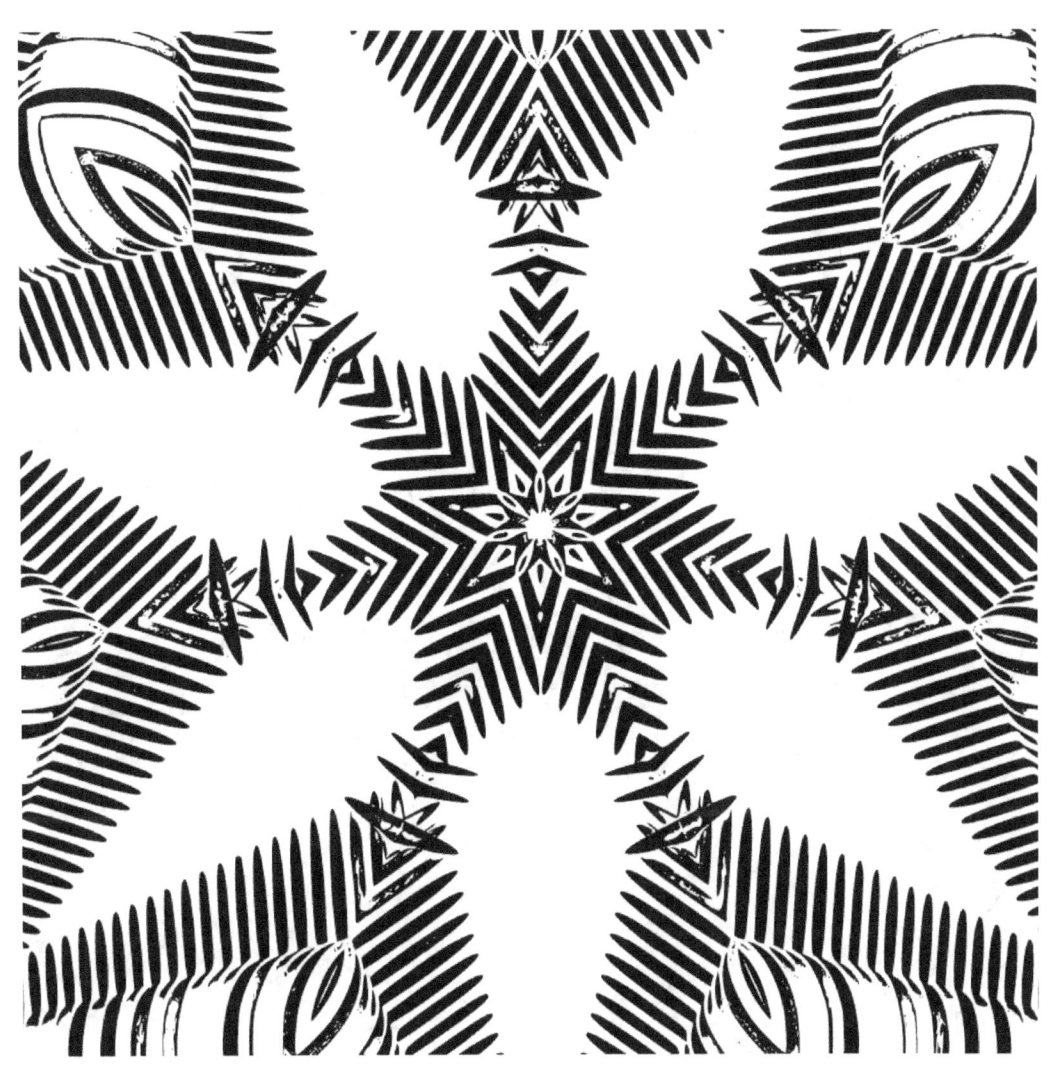

MANDALA
ART

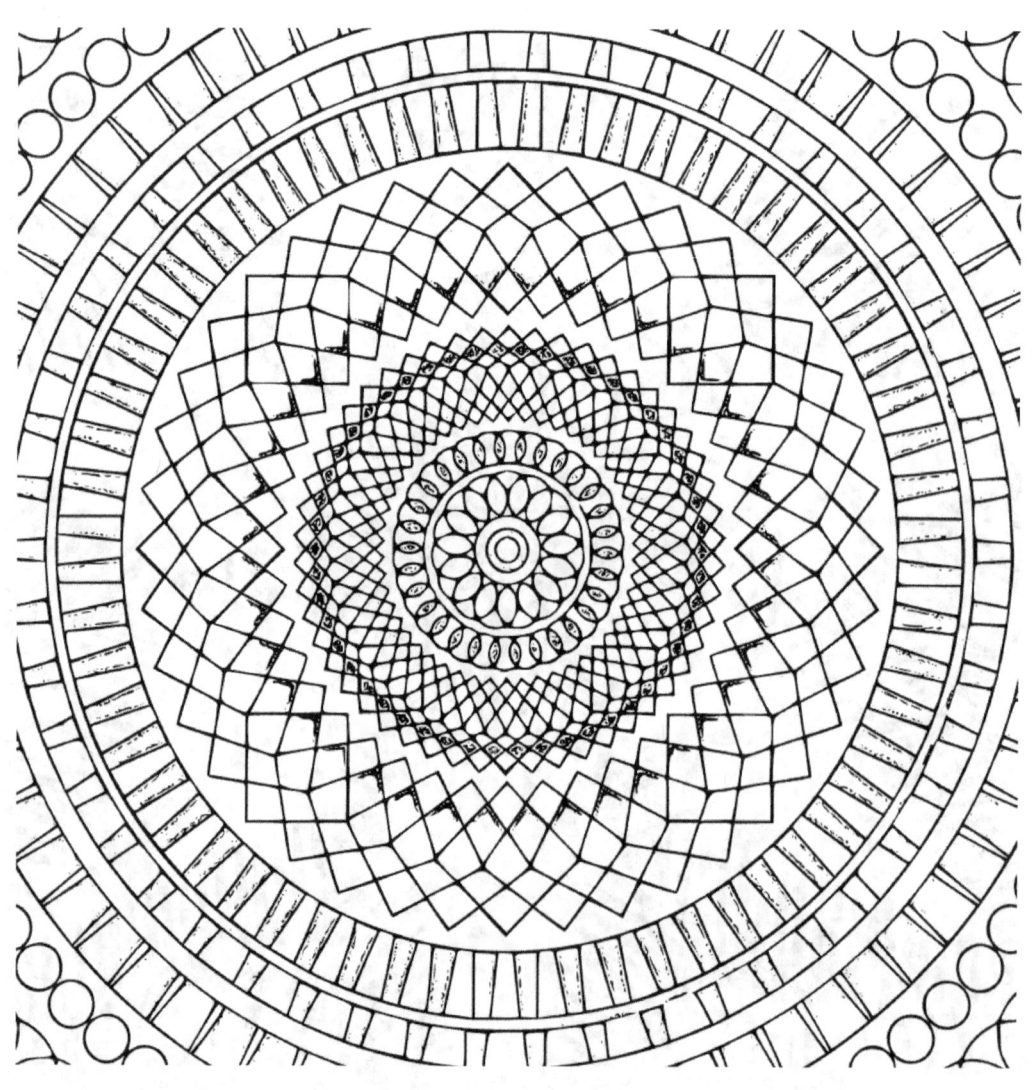

MANDALA
ART

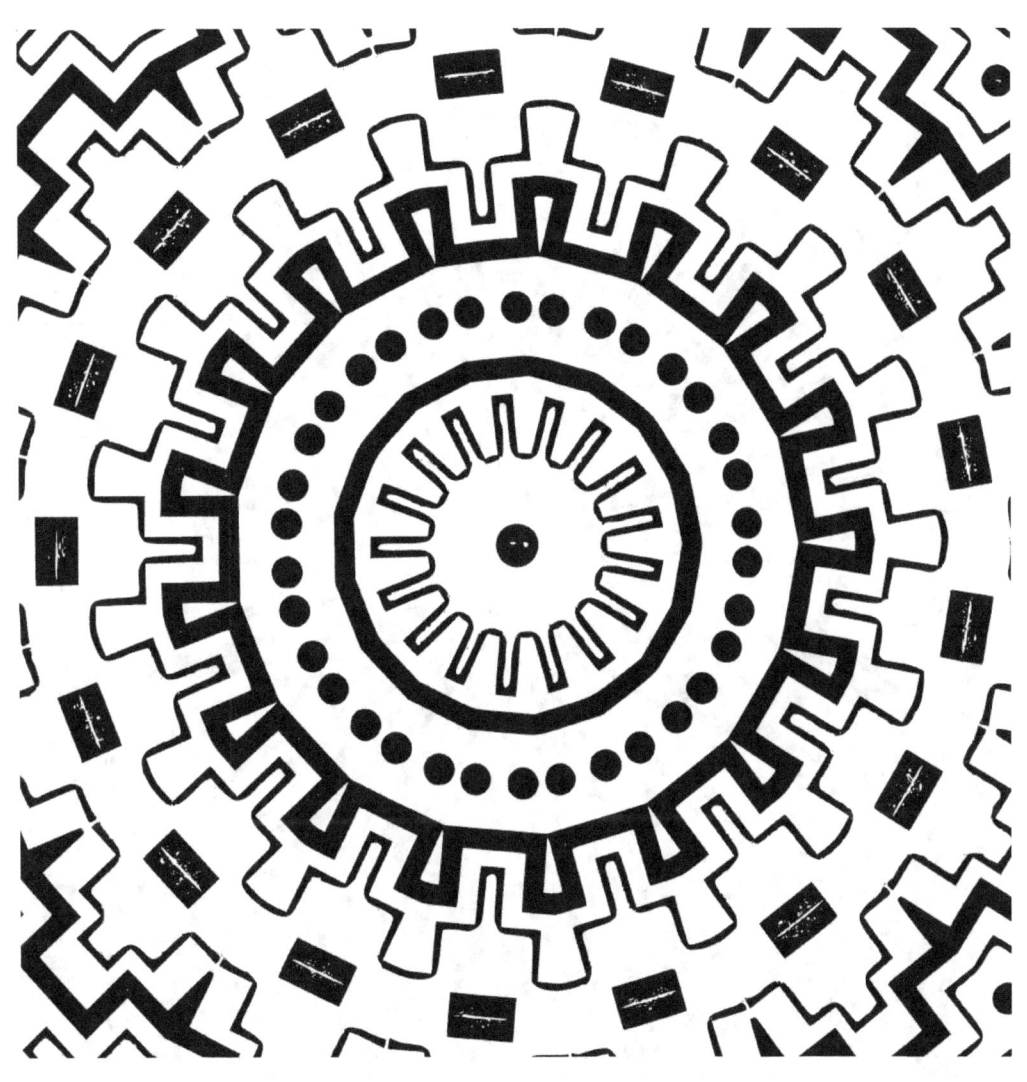

MANDALA
ART

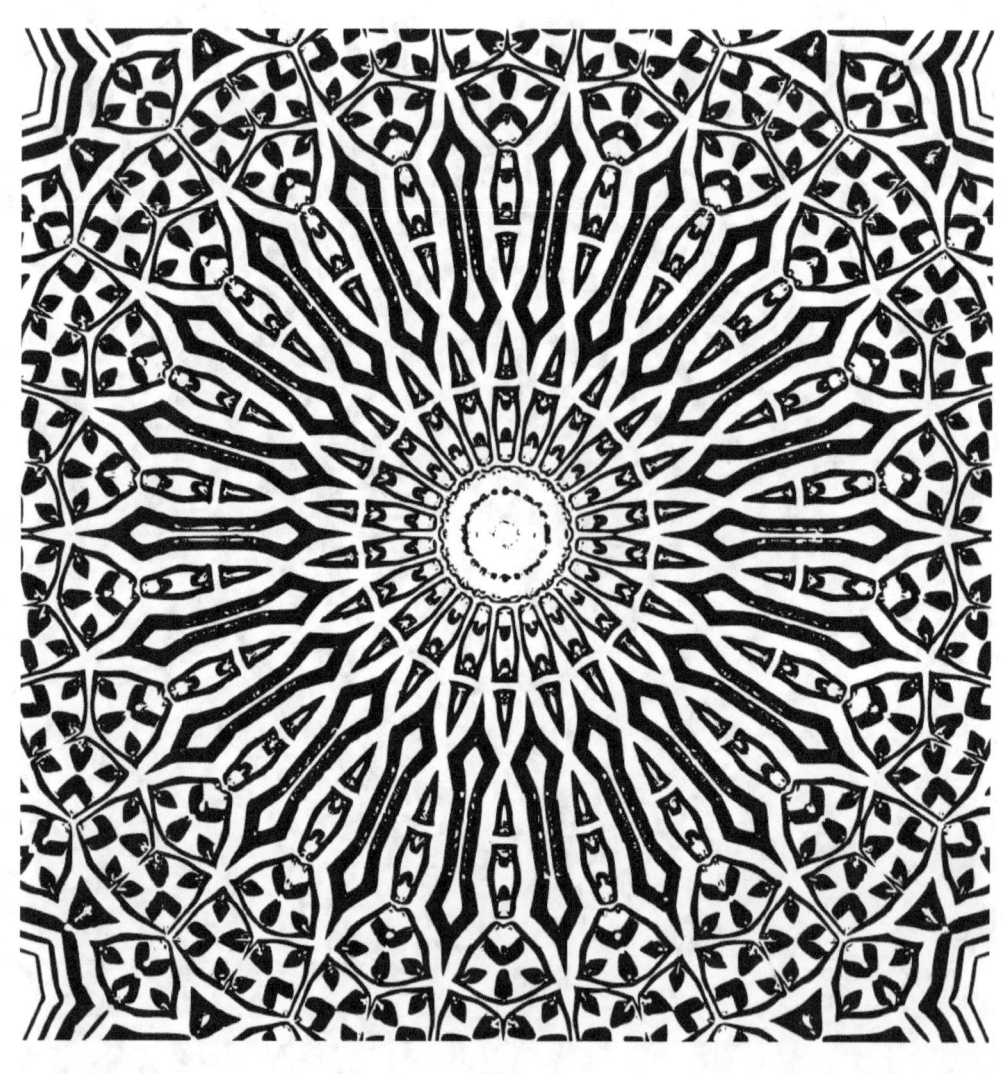

MANDALA
ART

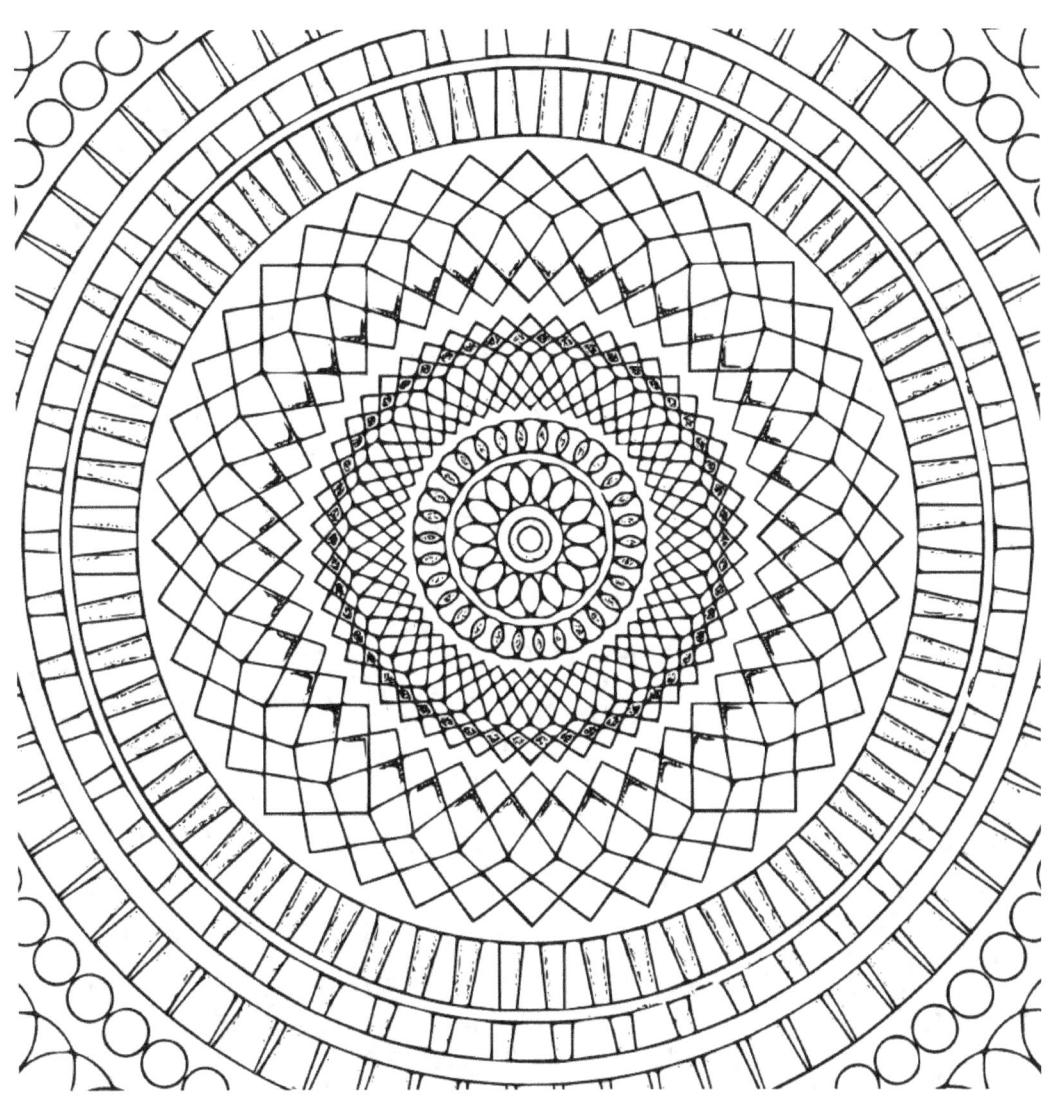

MANDALA
ART

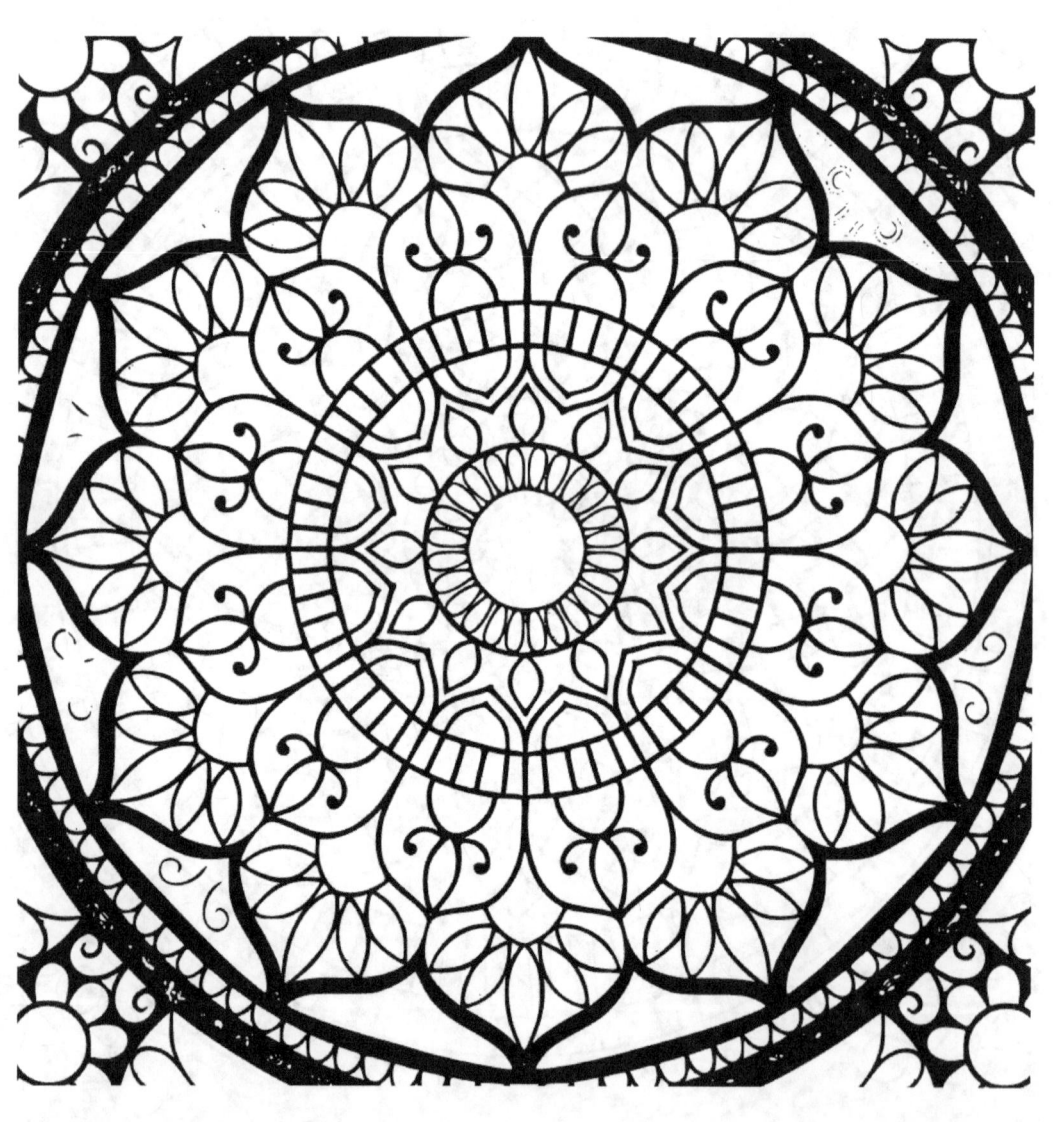

MANDALA
ART

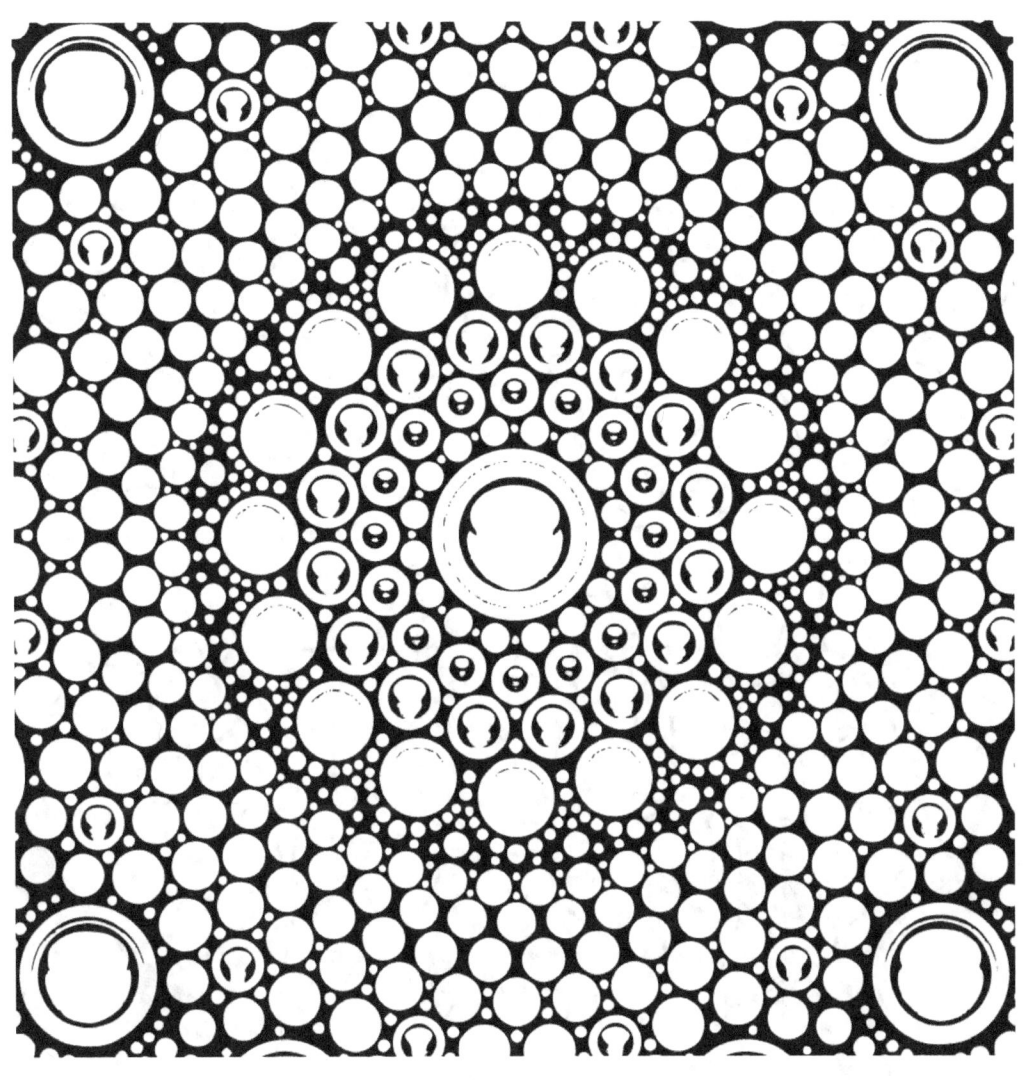

MANDALA
ART

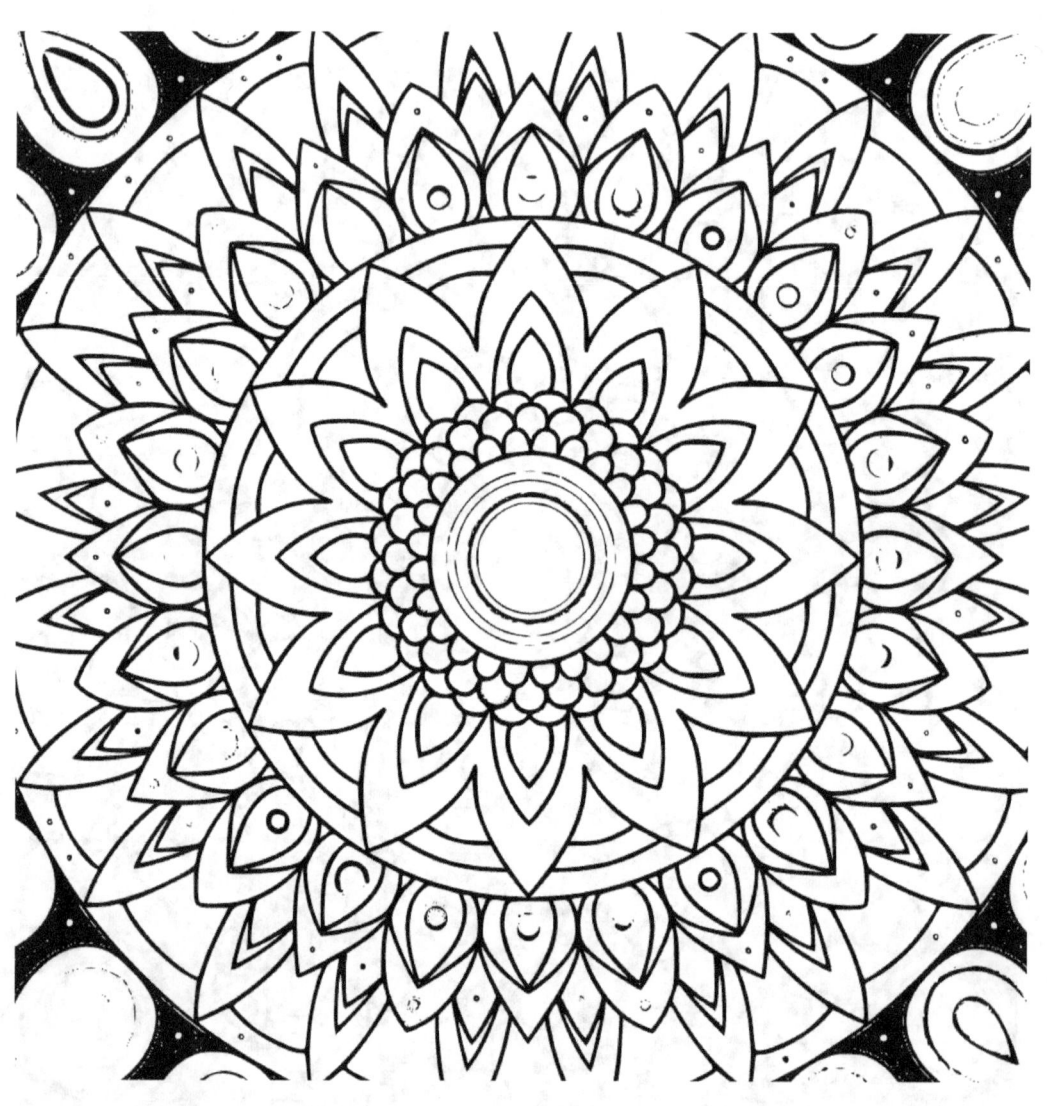

MANDALA
ART

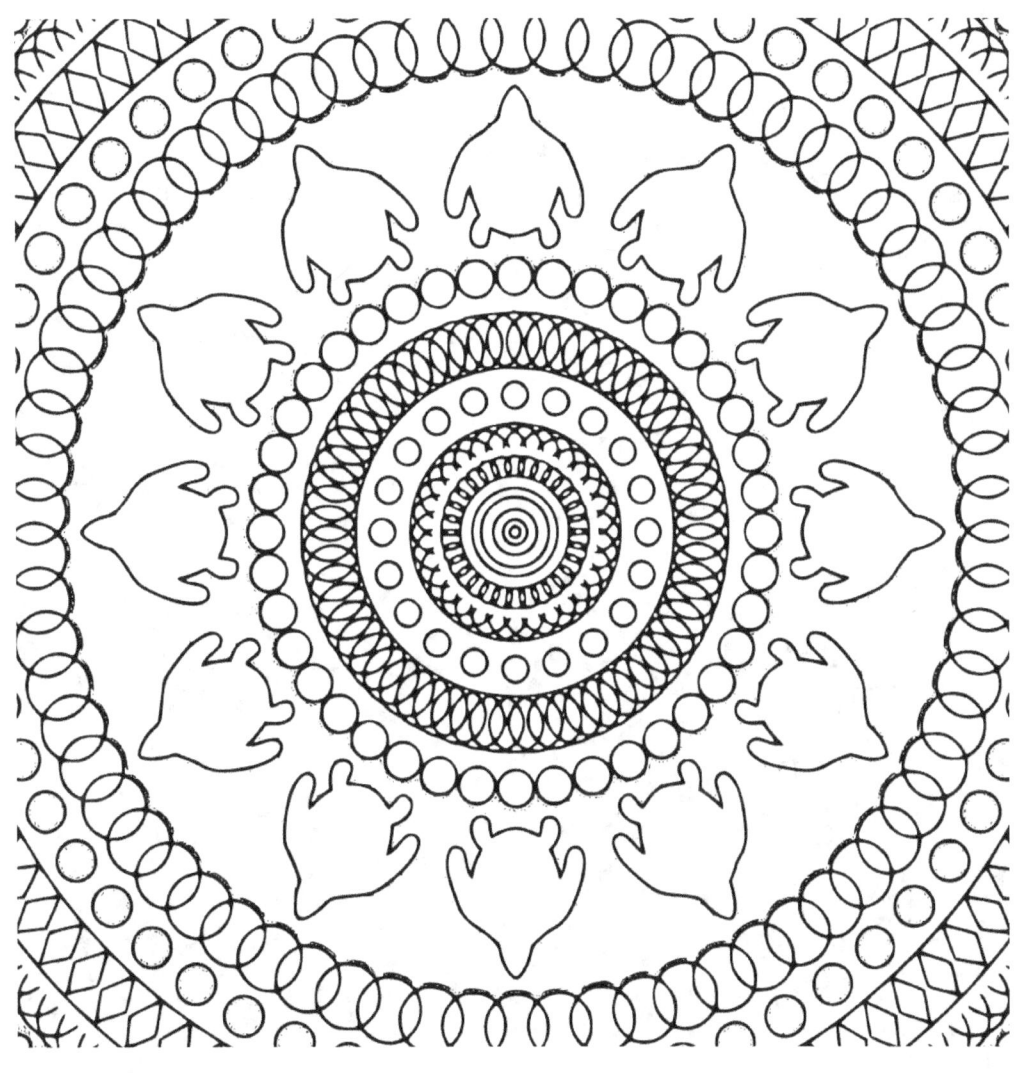

MANDALA
ART

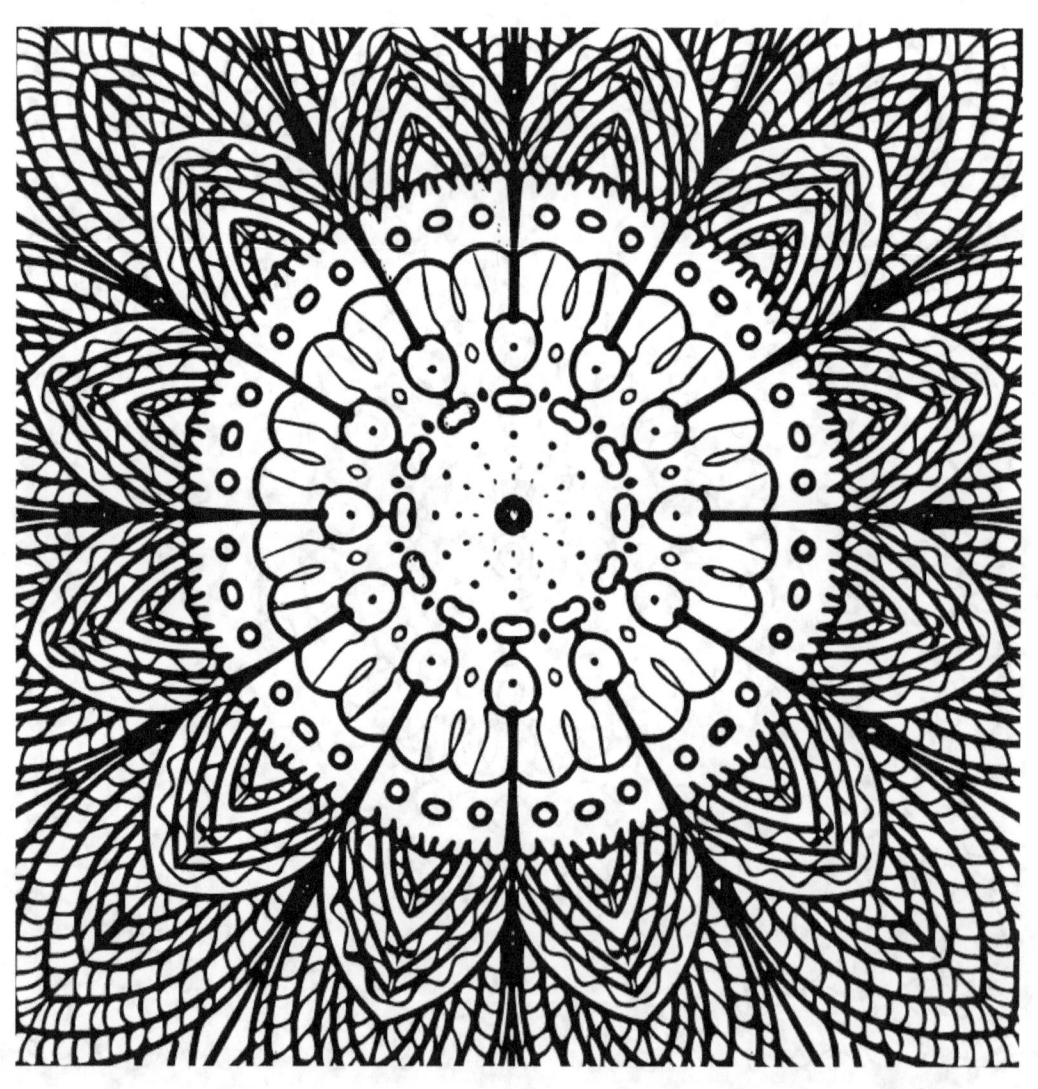

MANDALA
ART

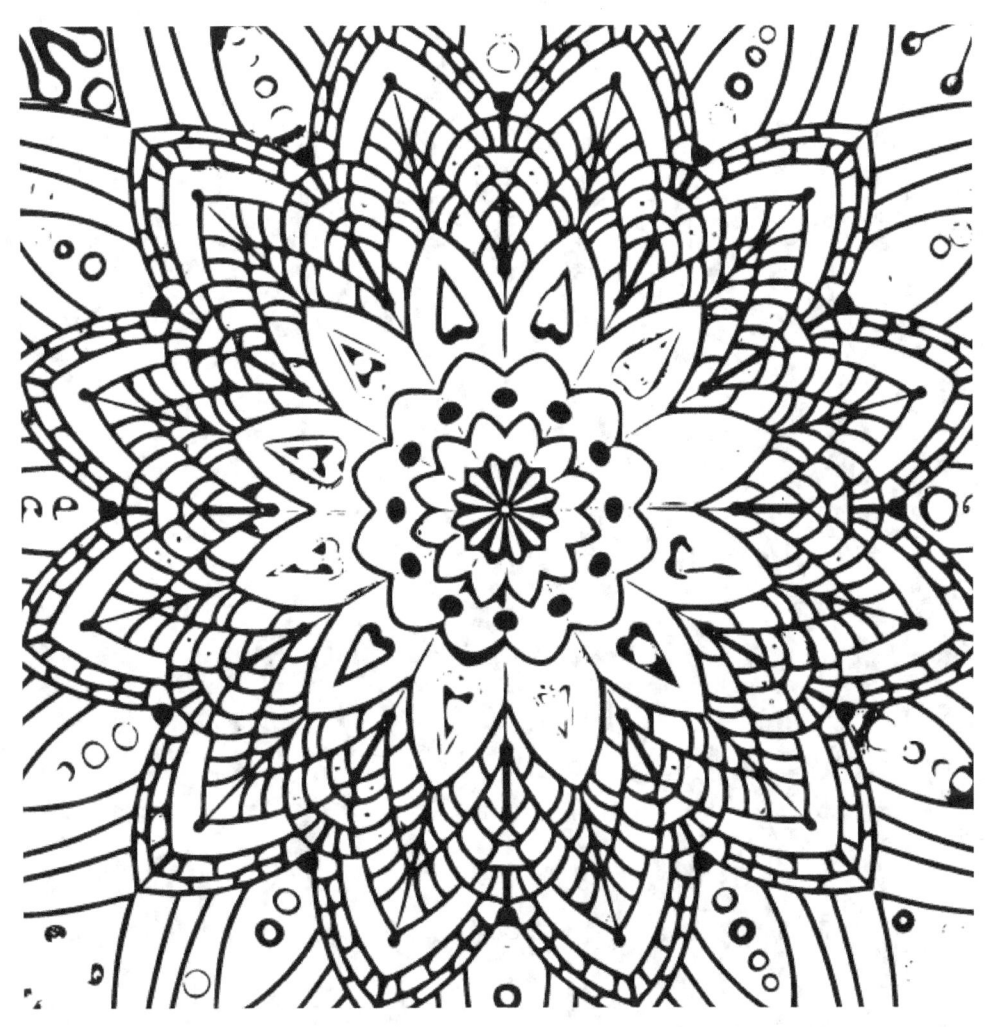

MANDALA

ART

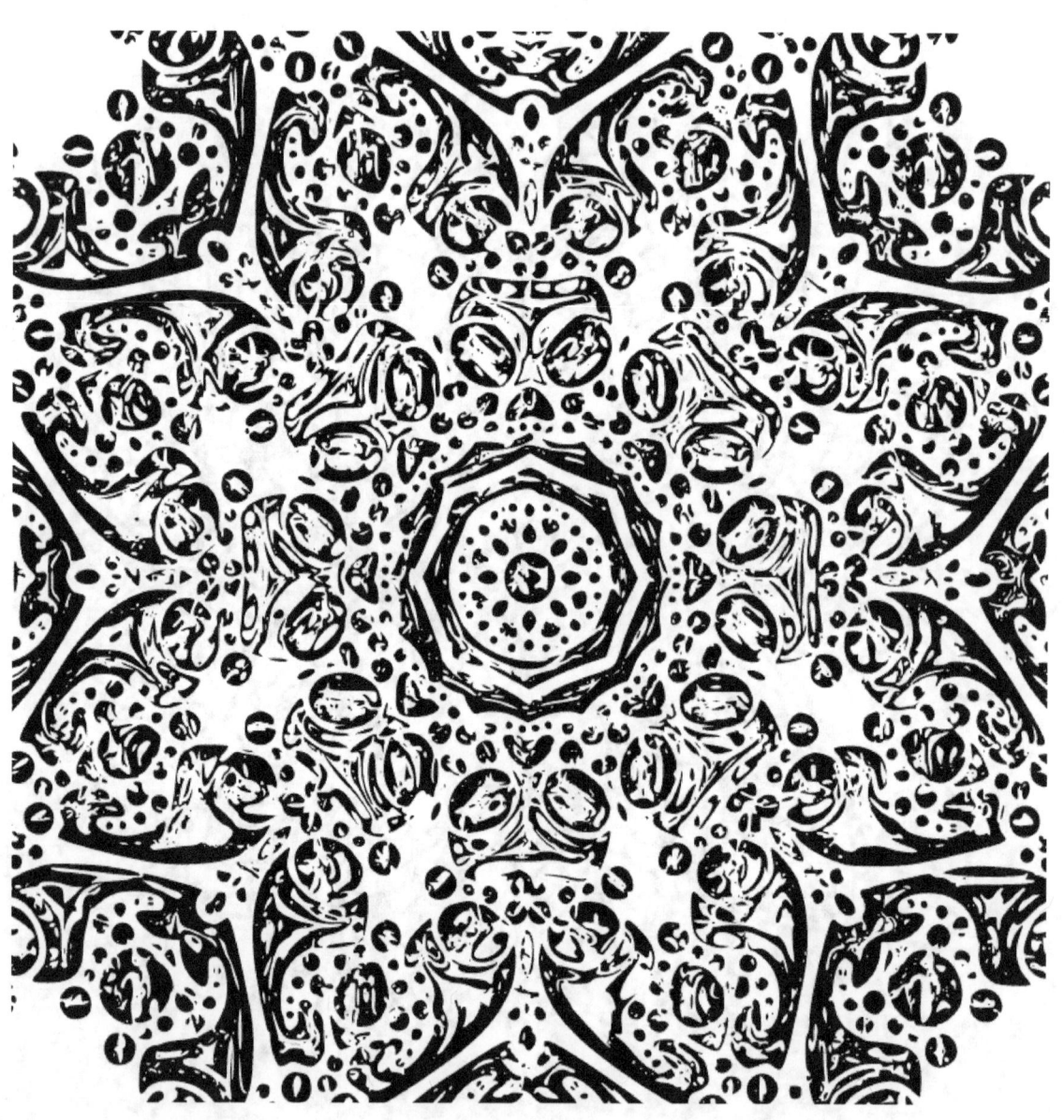

MANDALA
ART

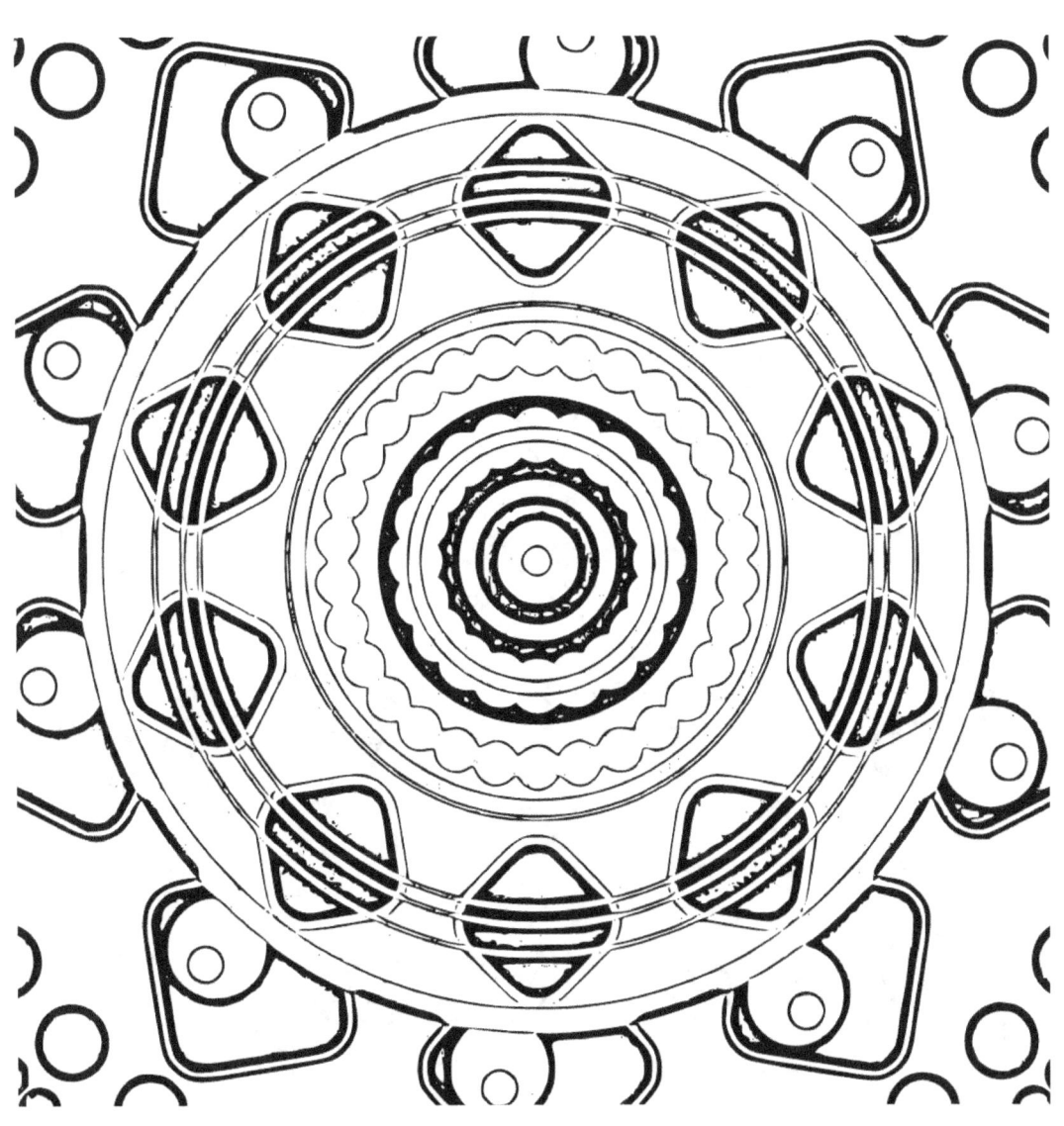

MANDALA
ART

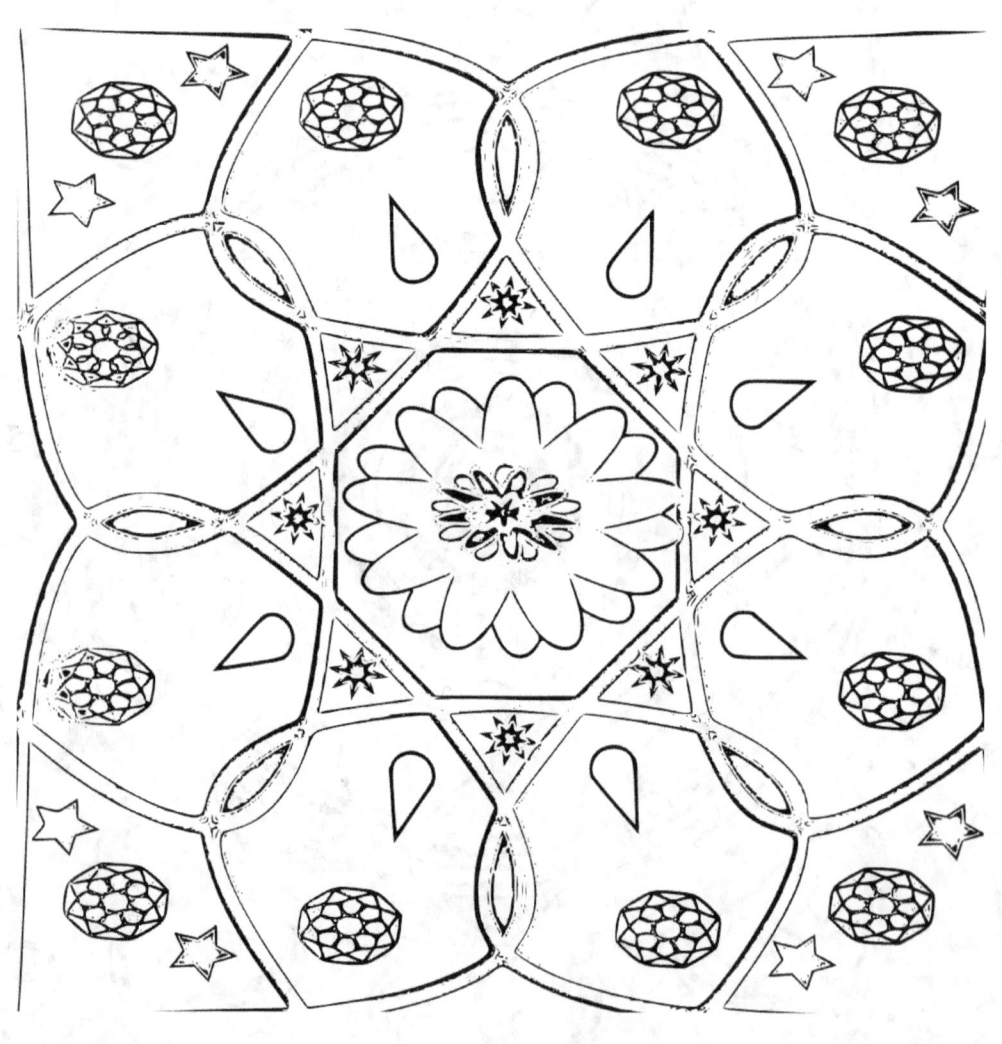

MANDALA
ART

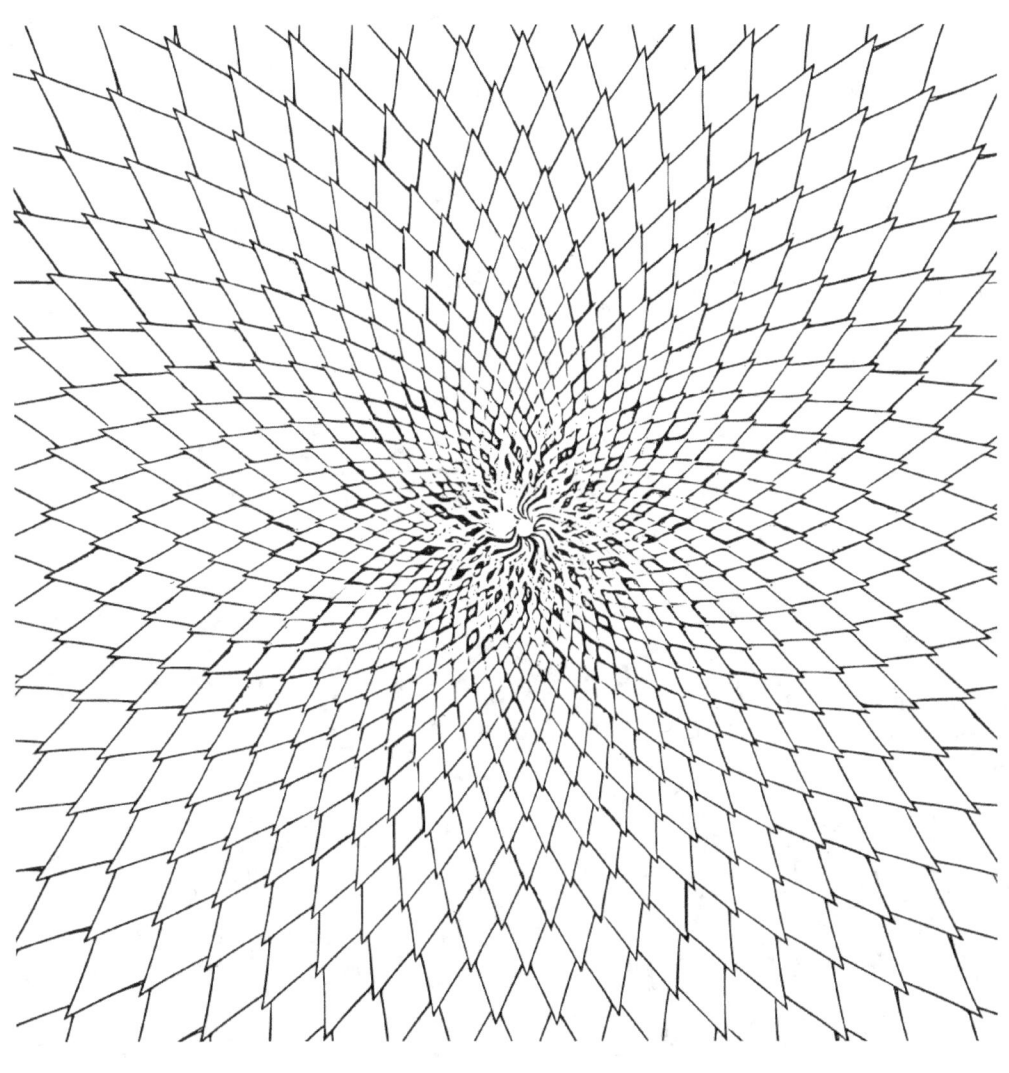

MANDALA
ART

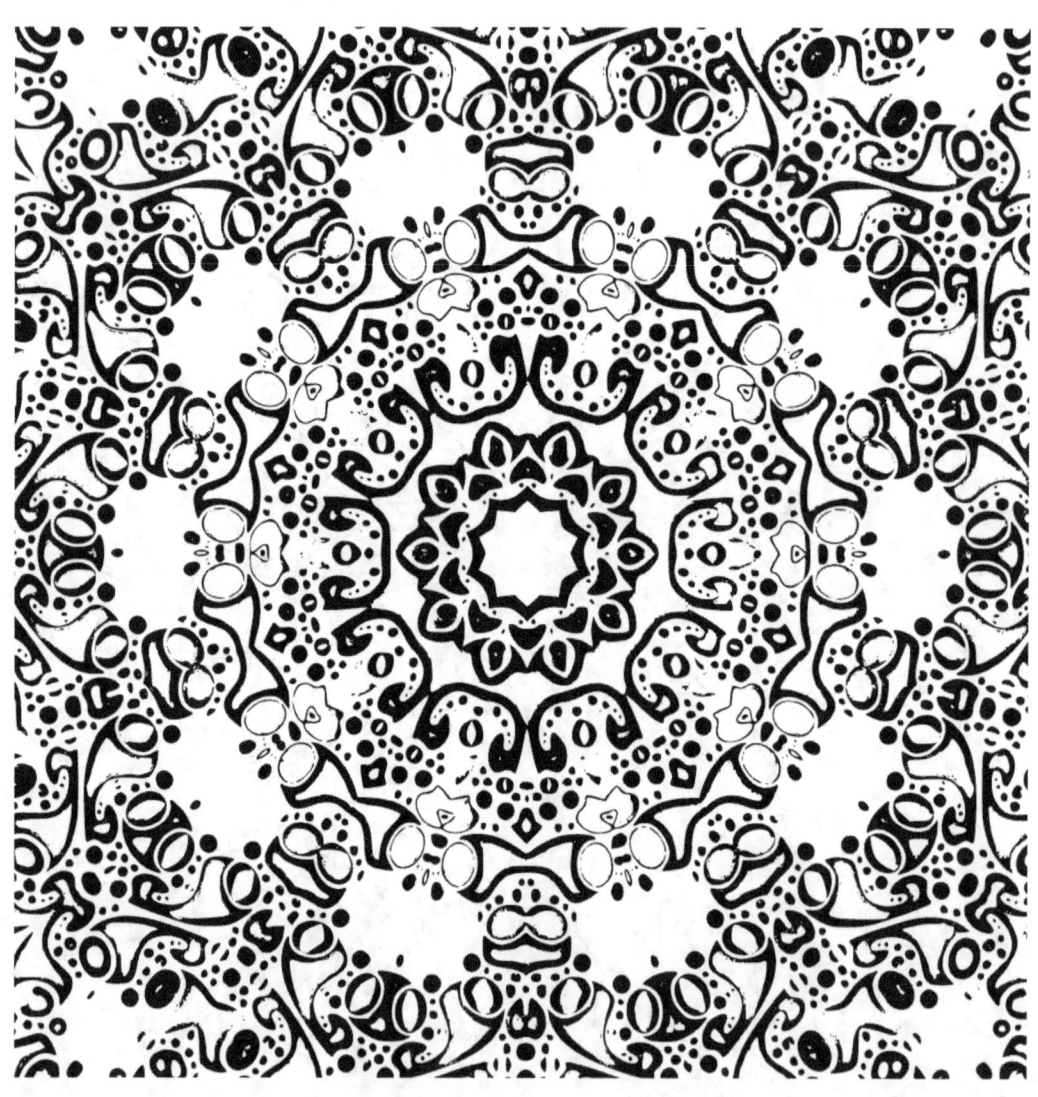

MANDALA
ART

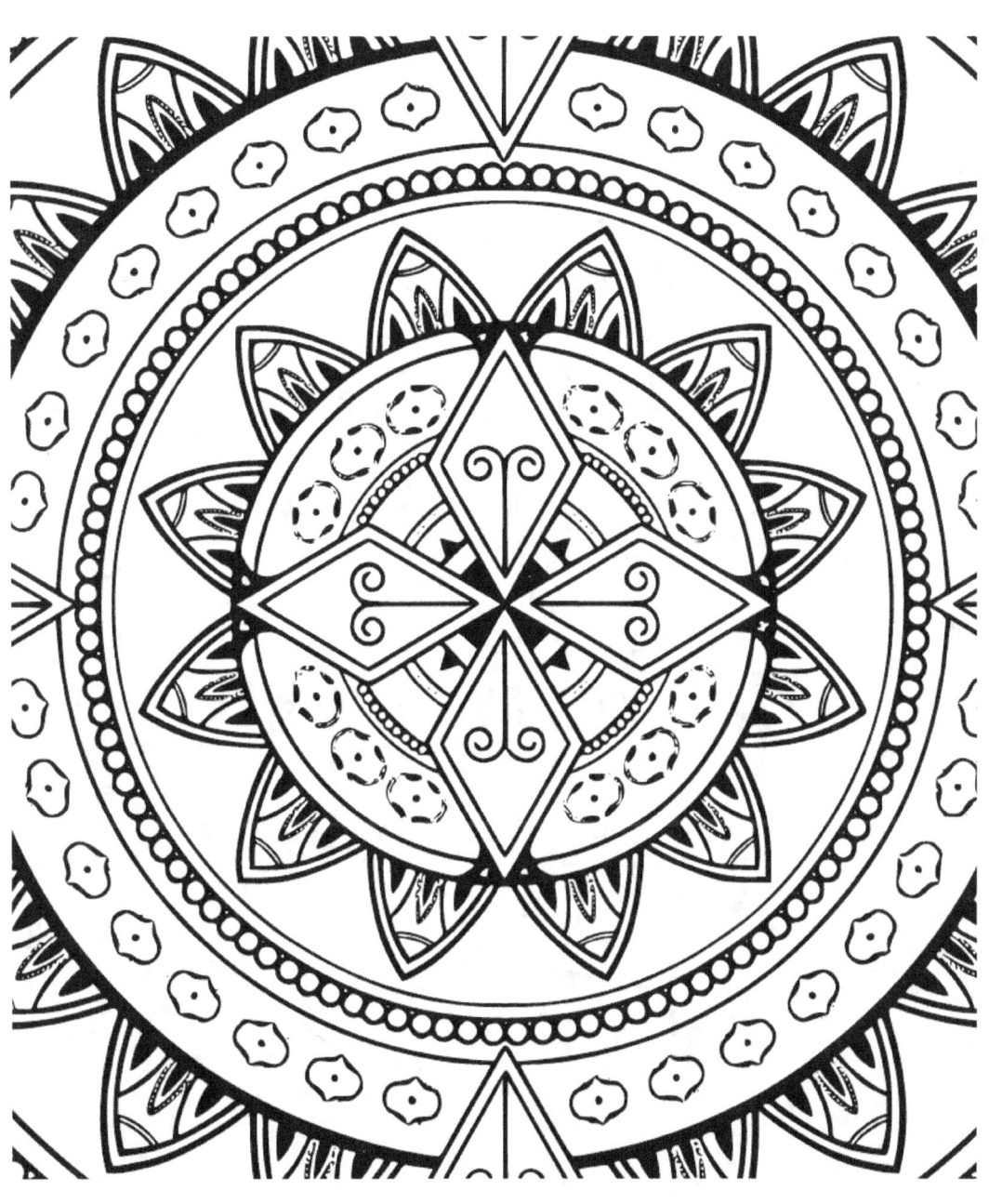

MANDALA
ART

MANDALA
ART

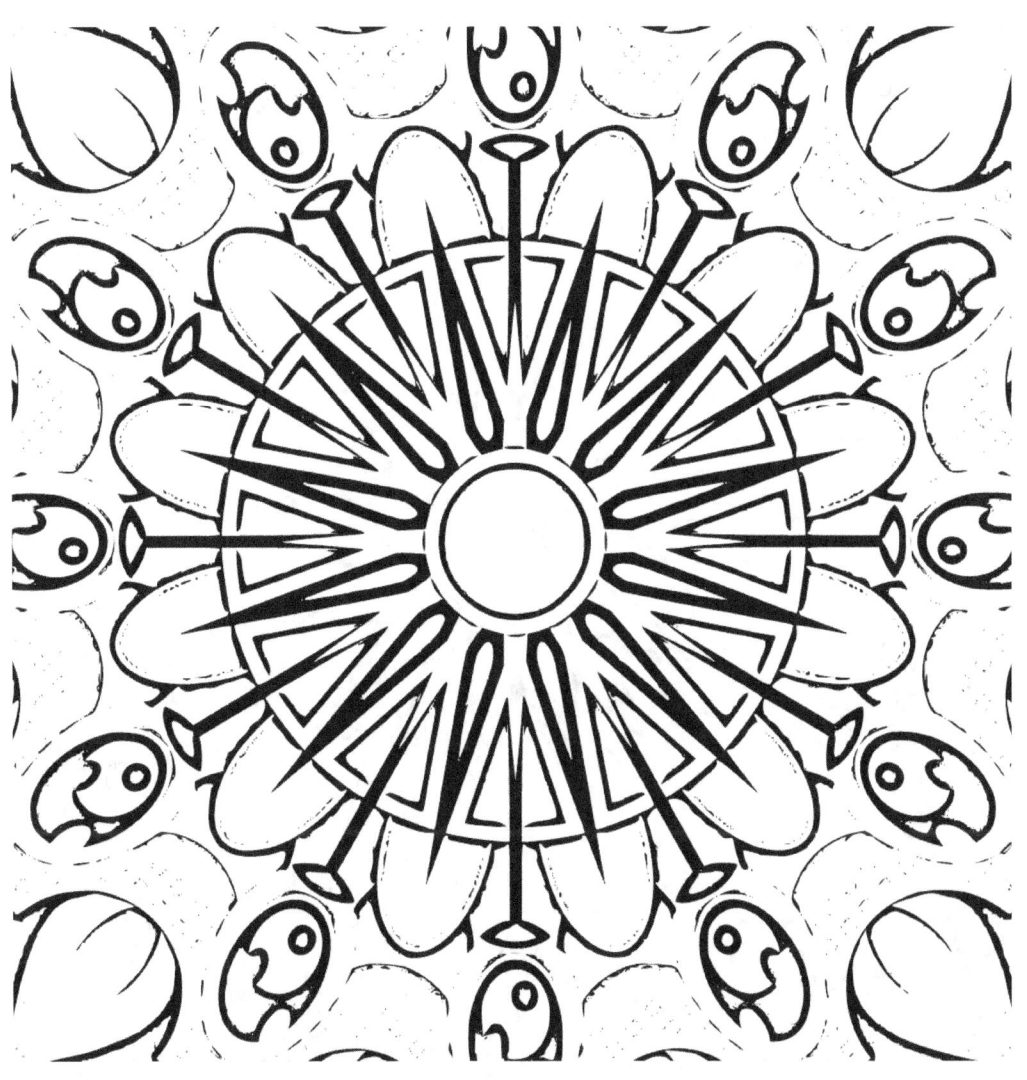

MANDALA
ART

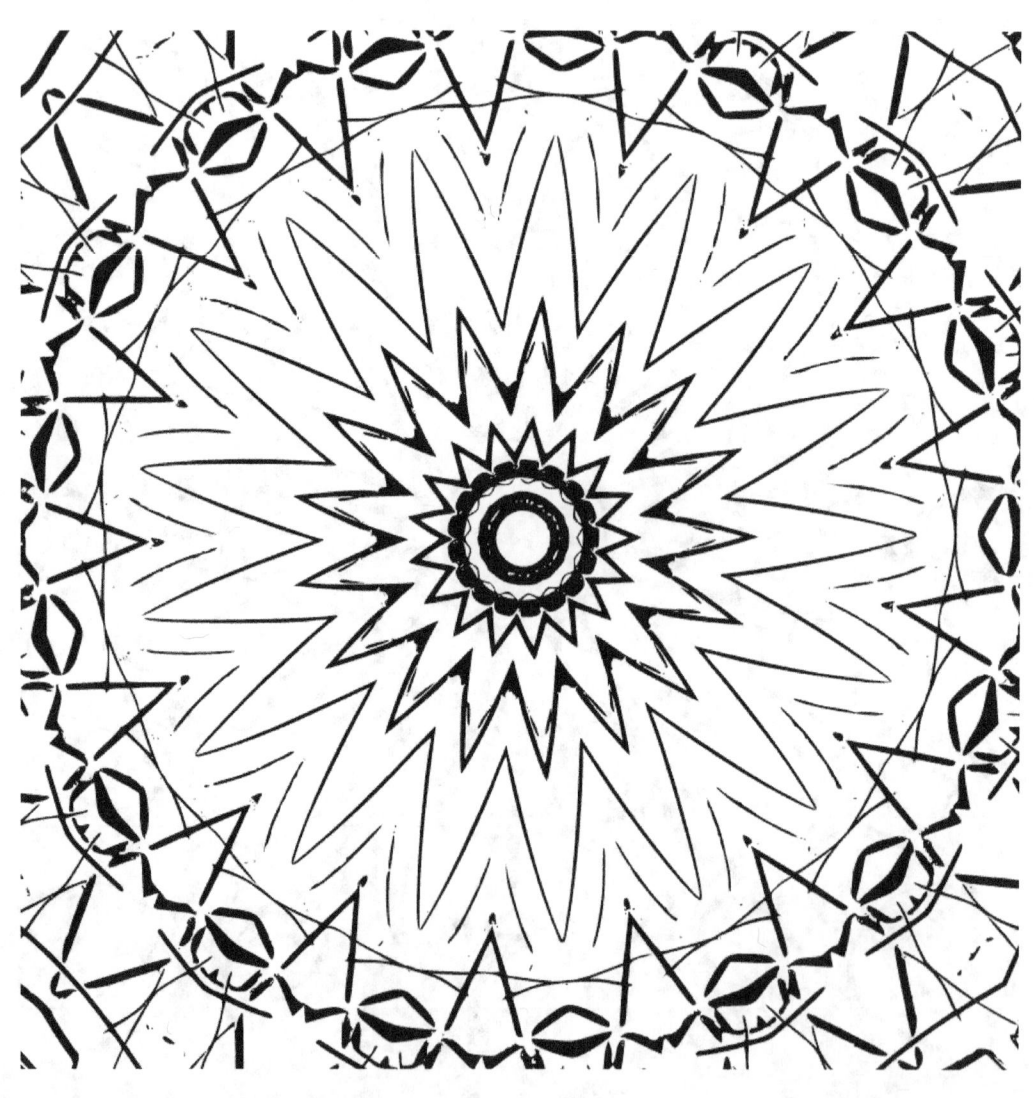

MANDALA

ART

MANDALA
ART

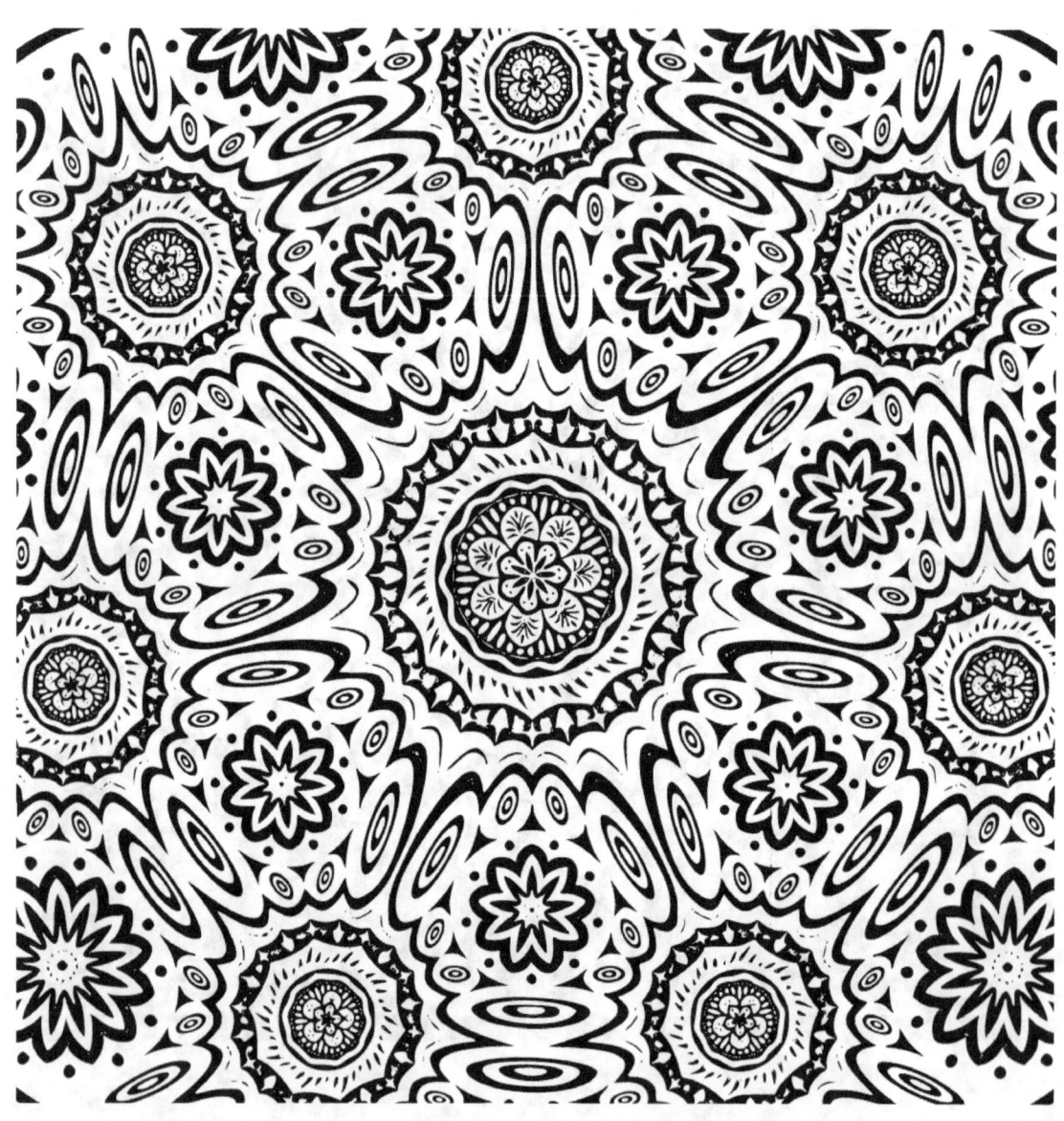

MANDALA
ART

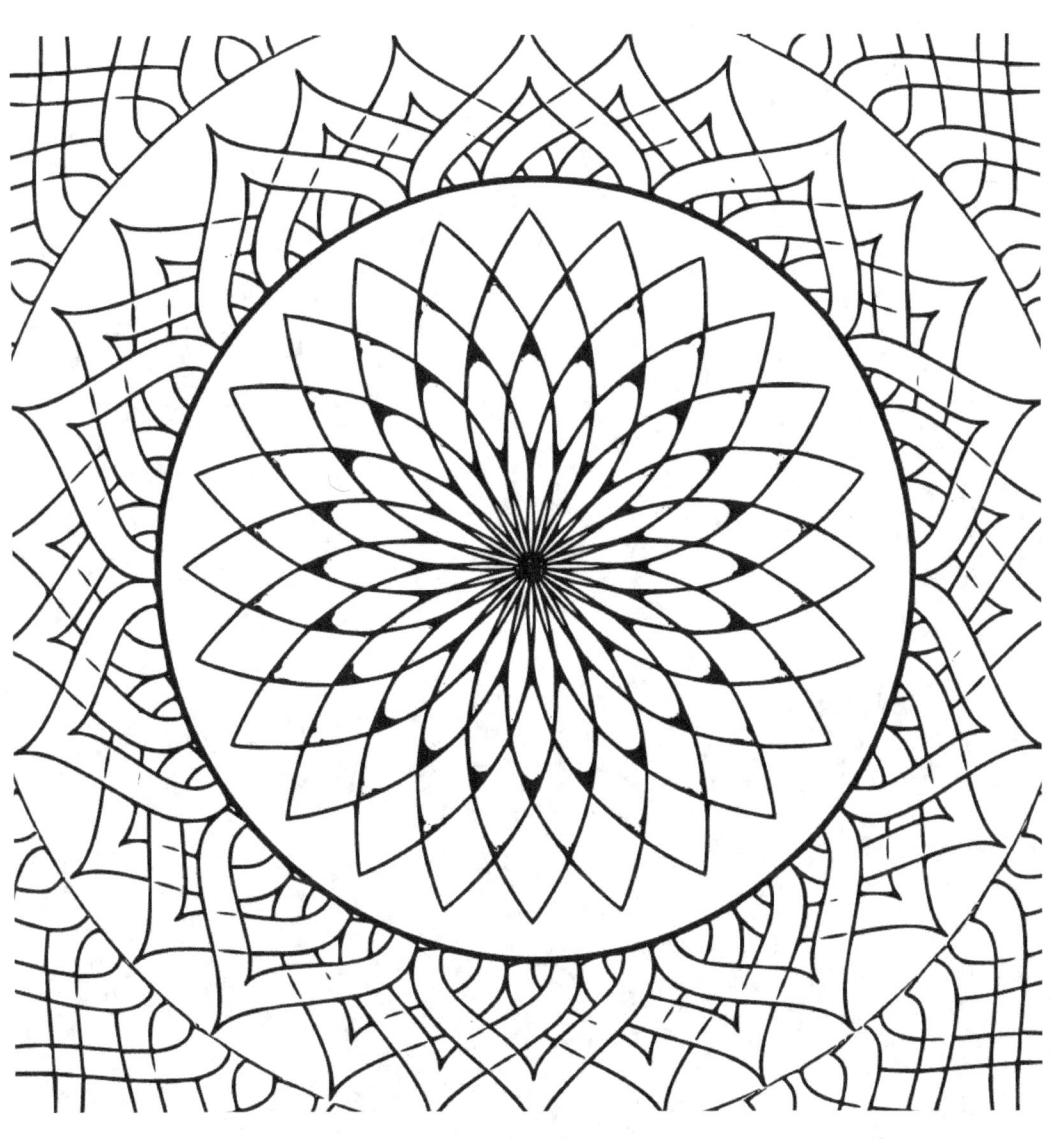

MANDALA
ART

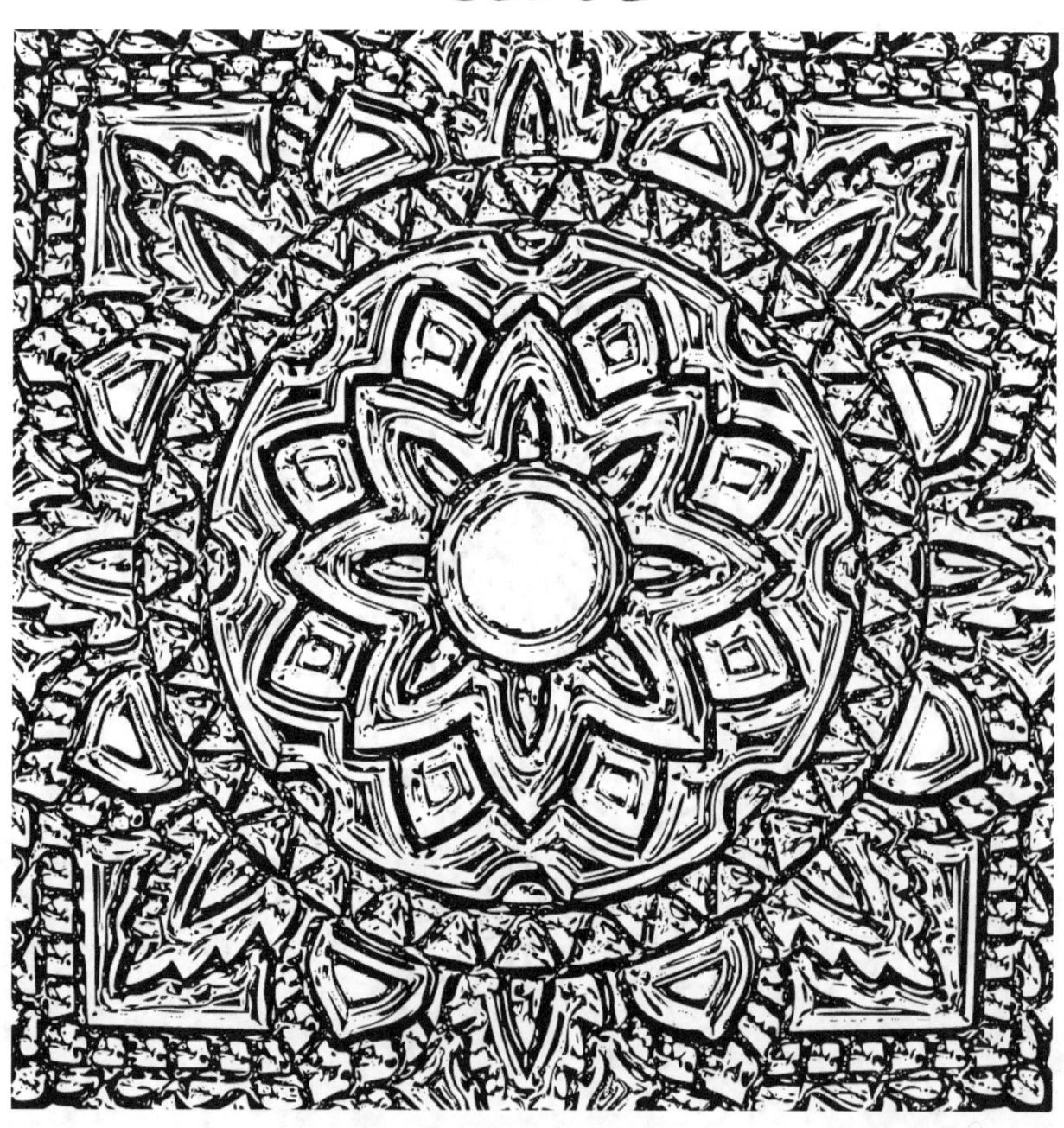

MANDALA

ART

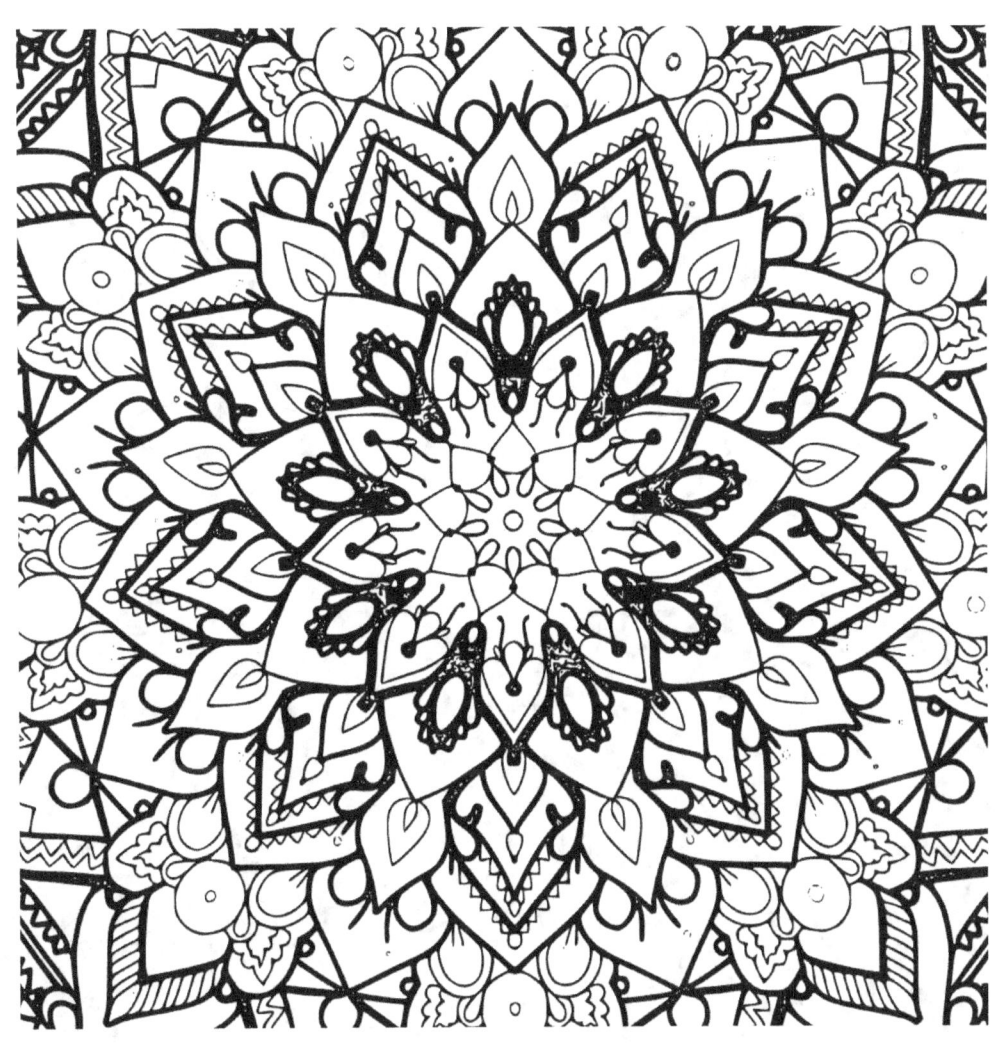

MANDALA
ART

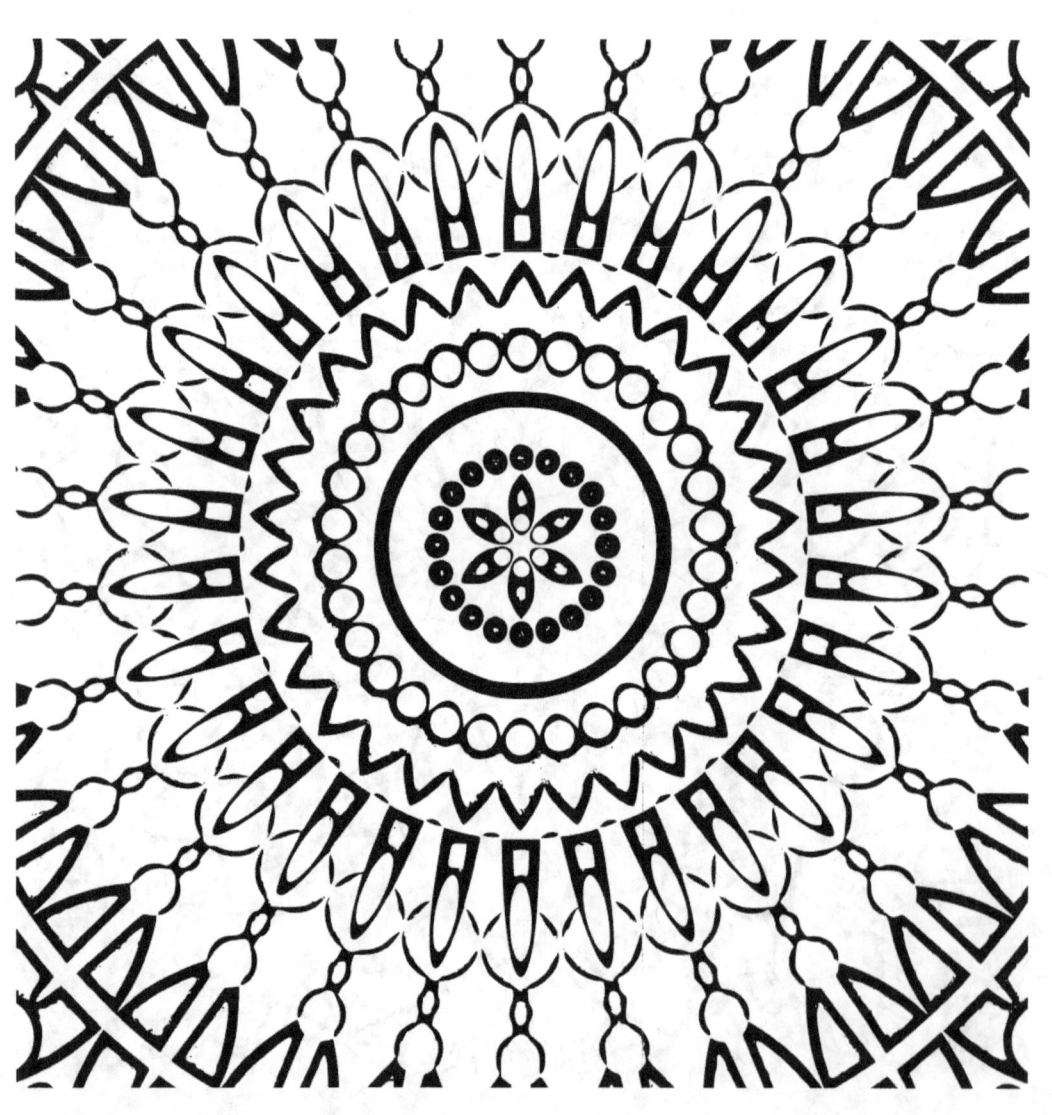

MANDALA

ART

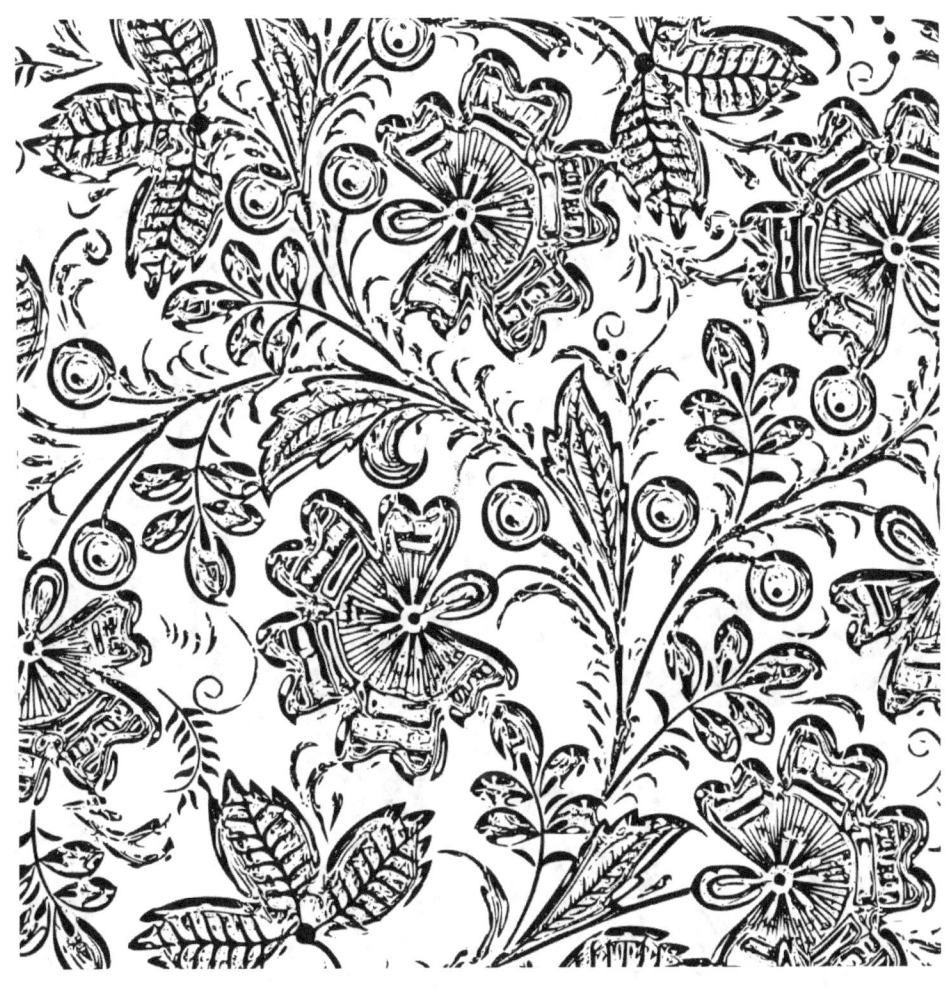

MANDALA
ART

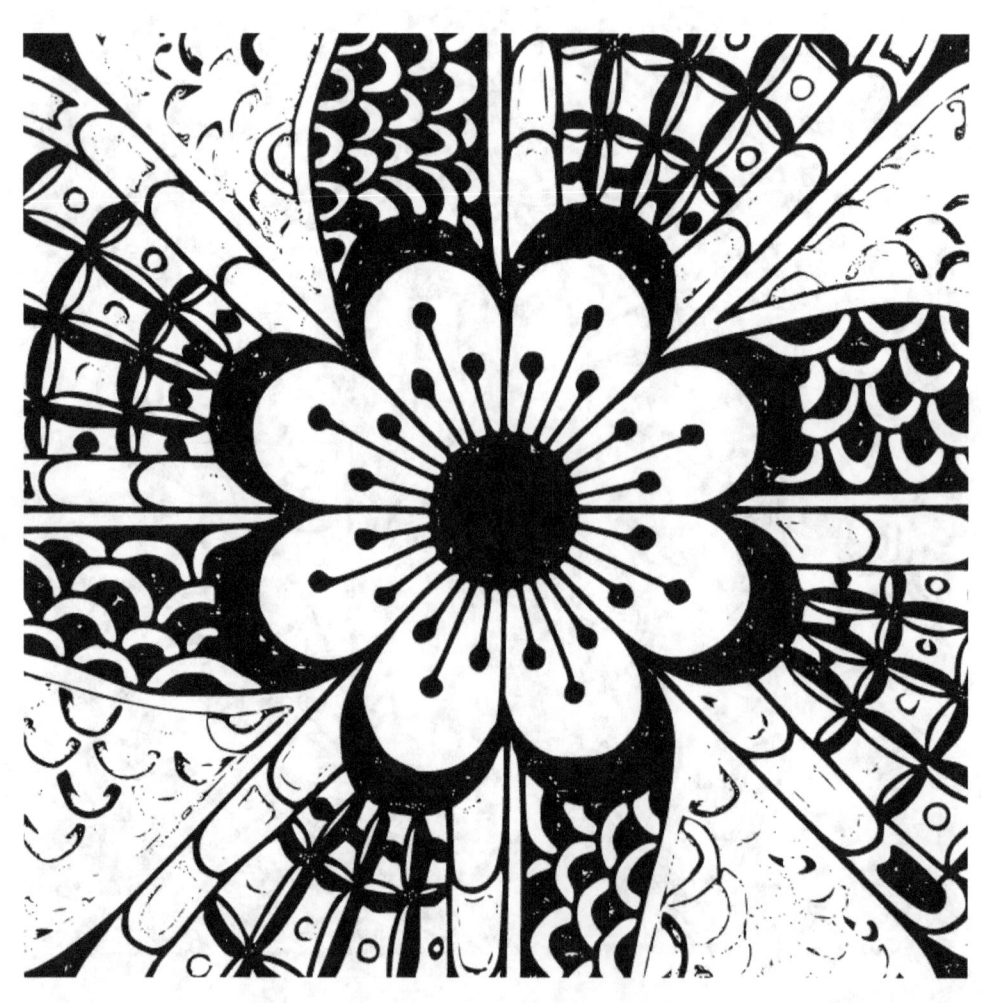

MANDALA
ART

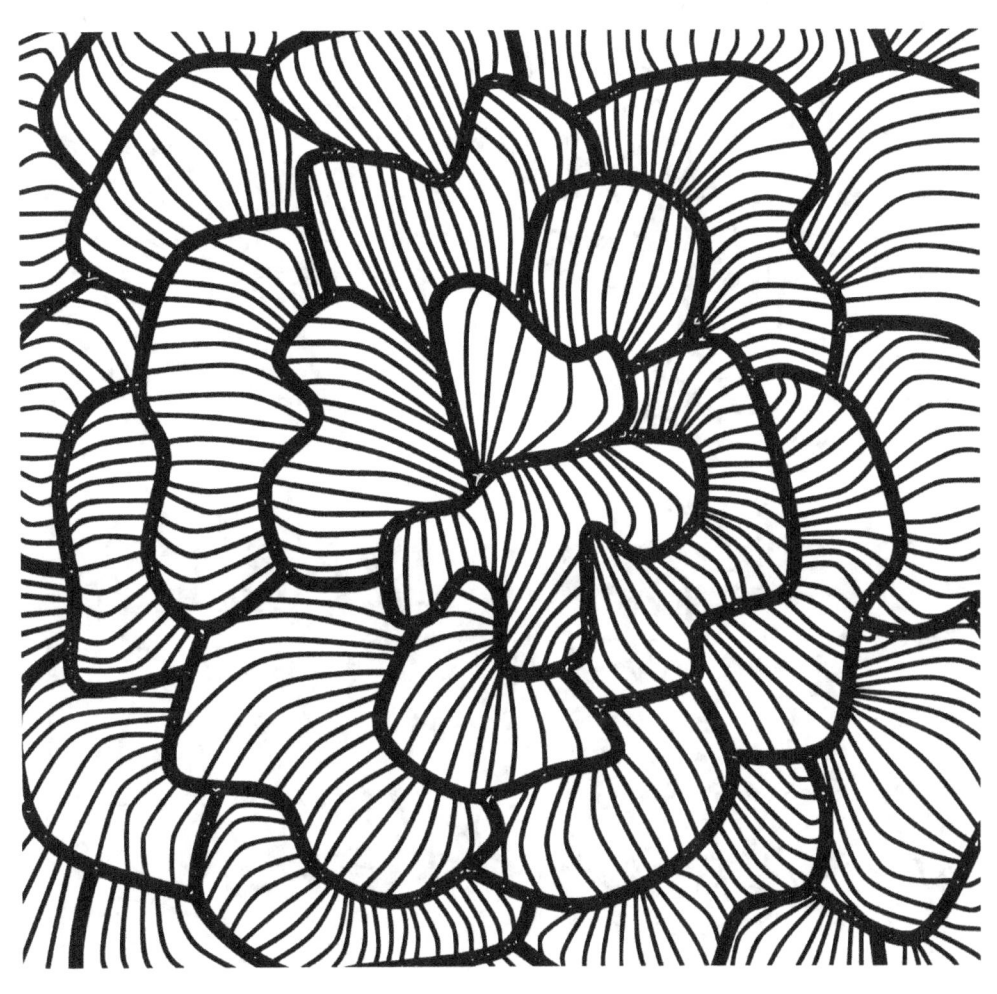

MANDALA
ART

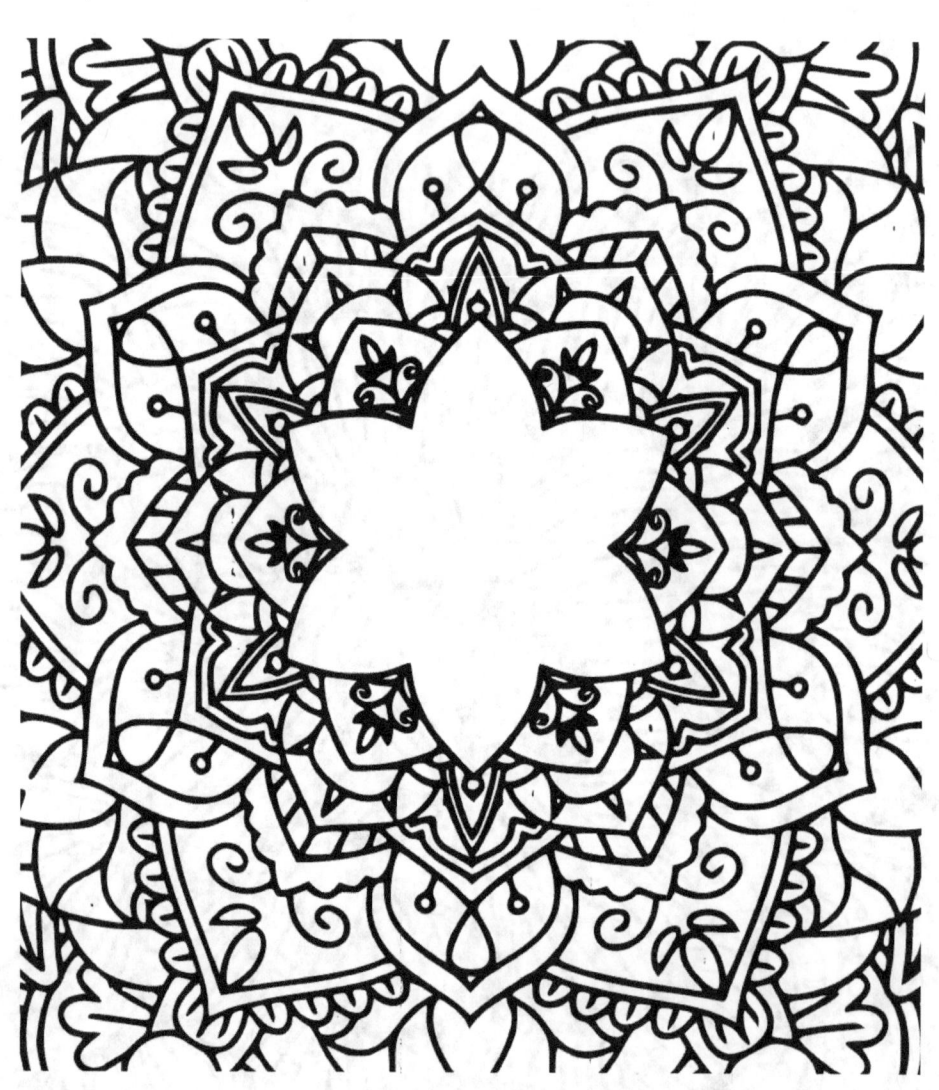

MANDALA
ART

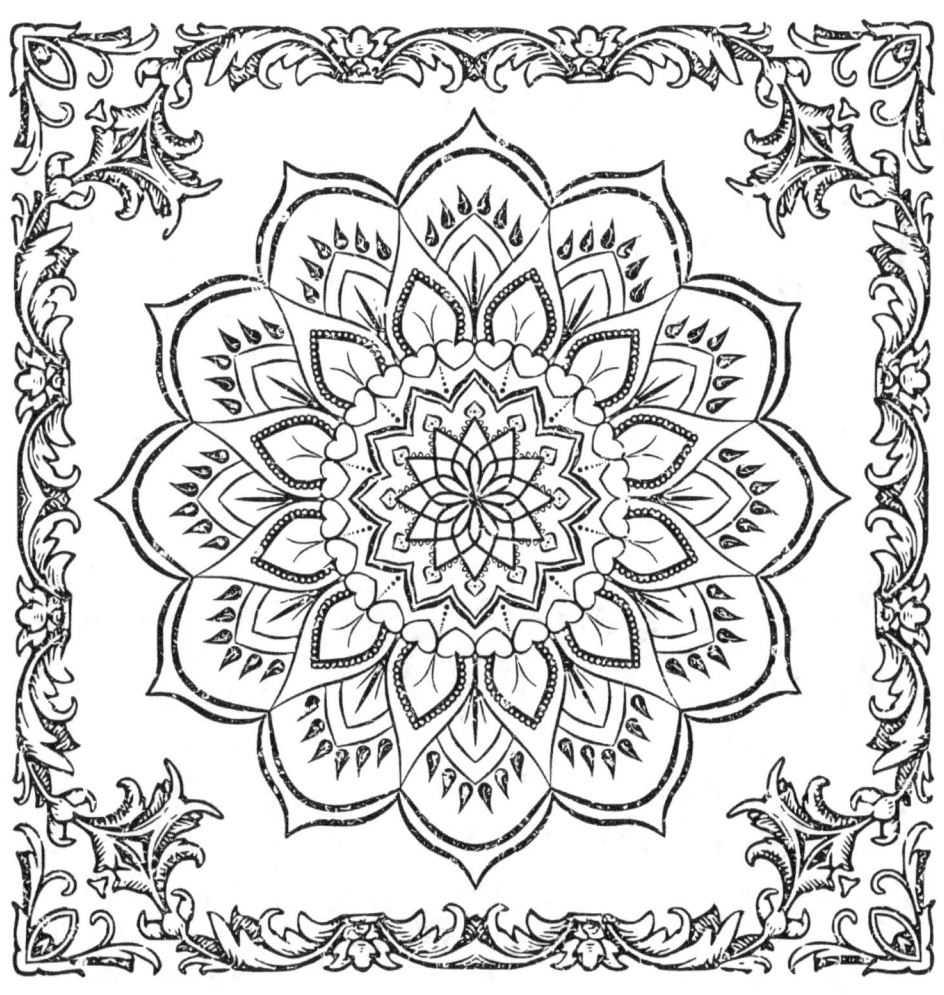

MANDALA
ART

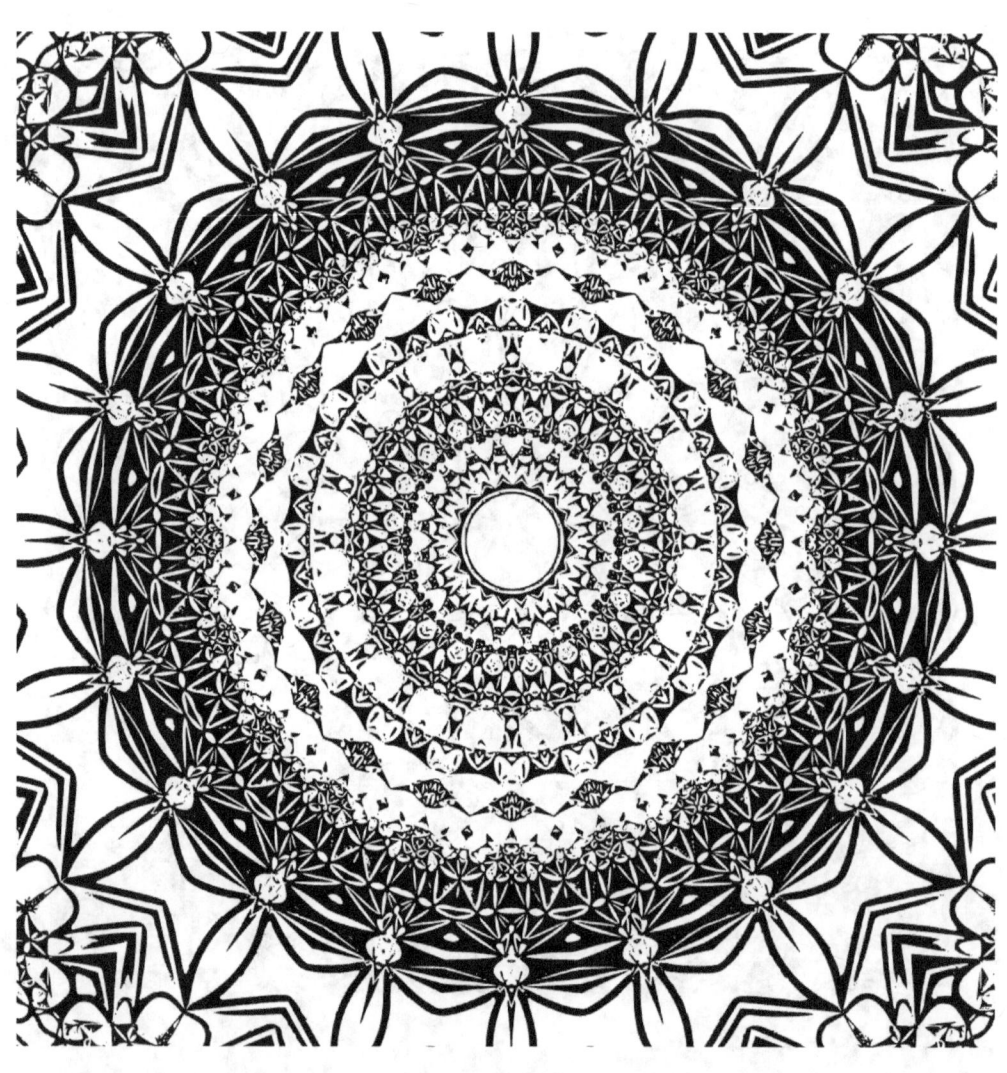

MANDALA

ART

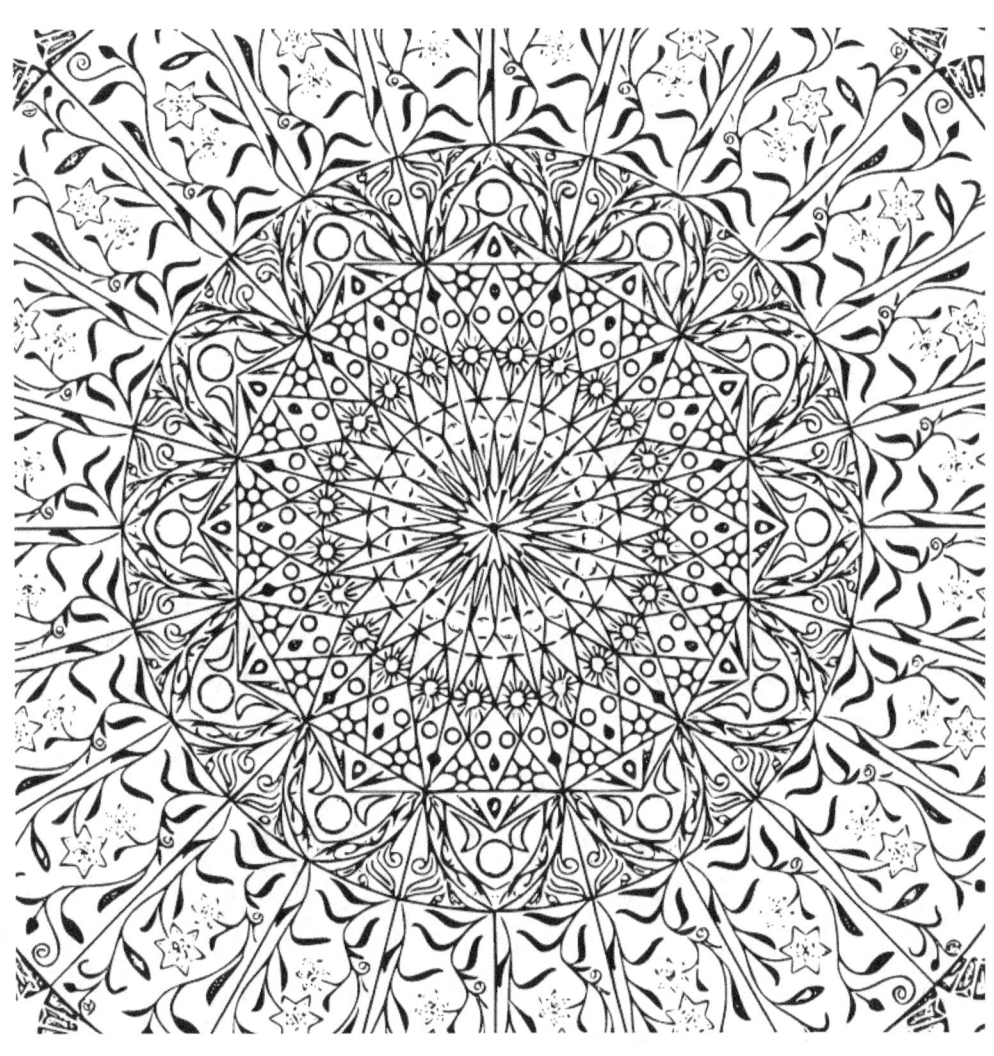

MANDALA
ART

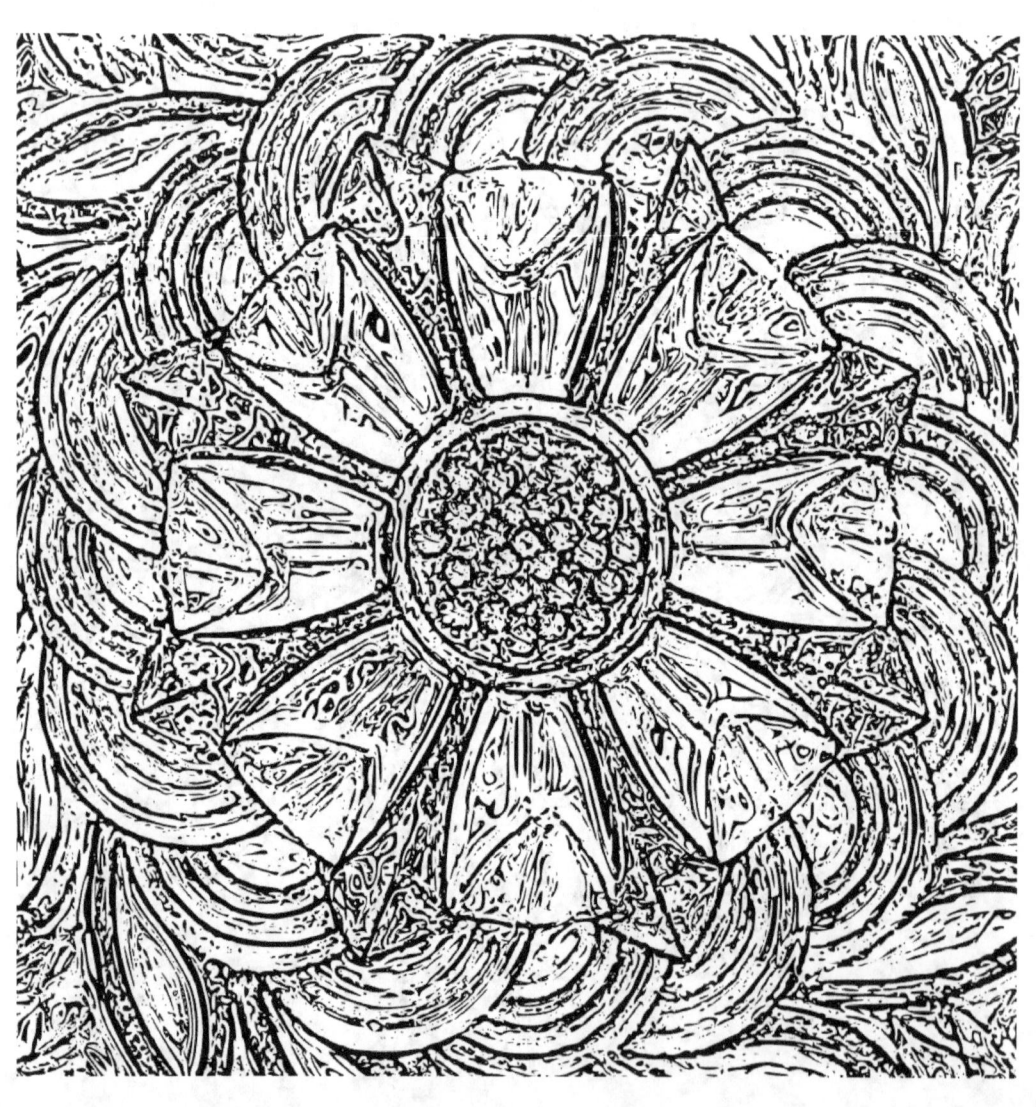

MANDALA
ART

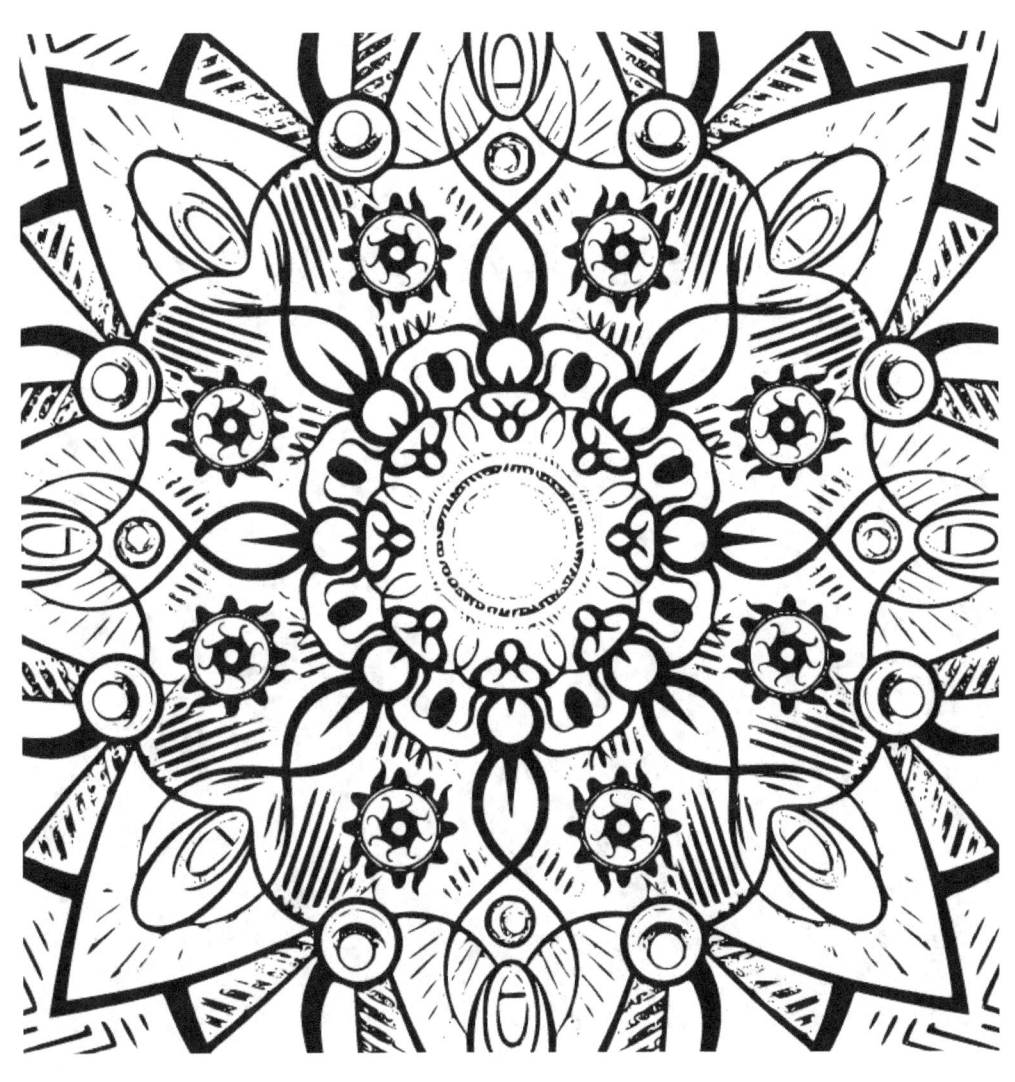

MANDALA
ART

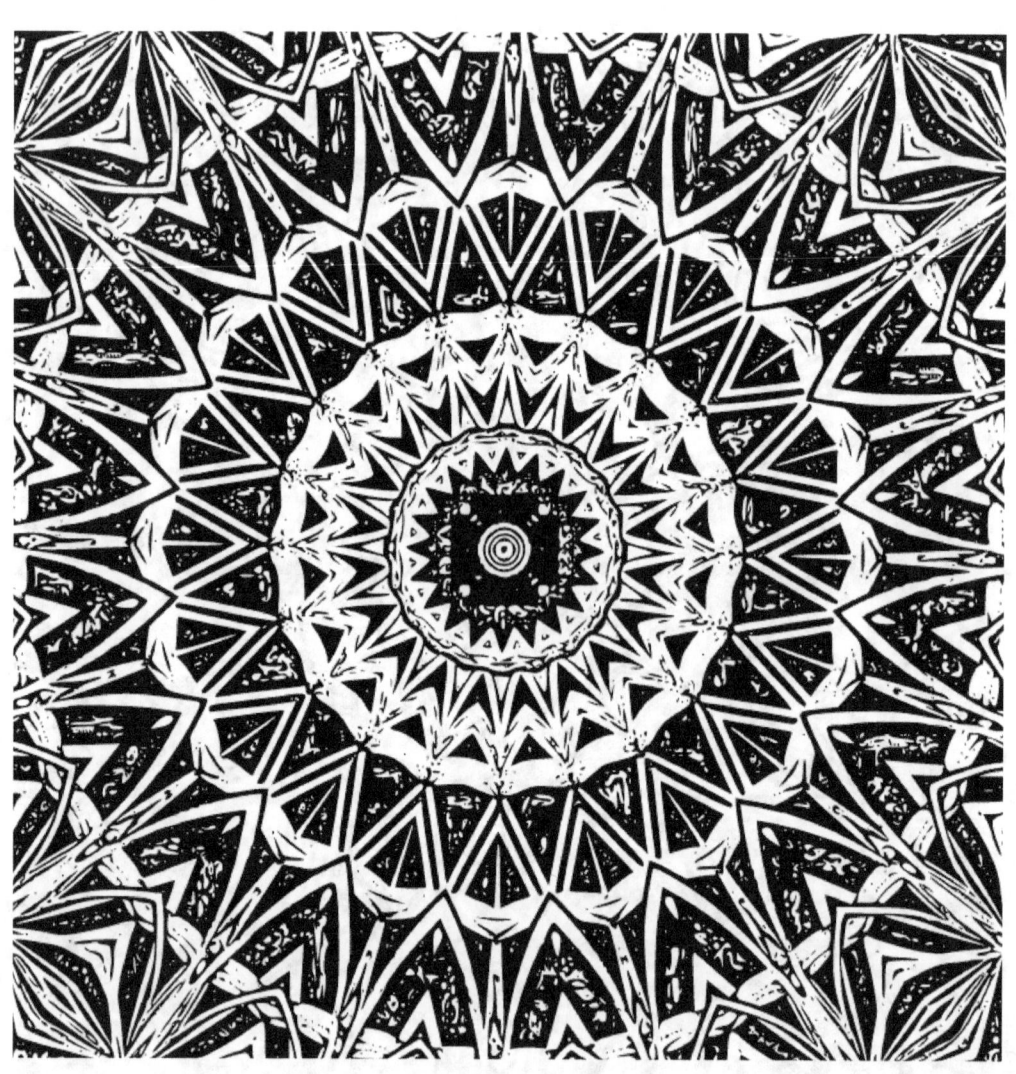